BUYING YOUR
FIRST FRANCHISE

by Rebecca R. Luhn, Ph.D.

THE
CRISP
SMALL BUSINESS &
ENTREPRENEURSHIP
SERIES

CREDITS

Editor: Nancy Shotwell

Layout/Design: ExecuStaff

Cover Design: Kathleen Gadway

Library of Congress 92-54355
ISBN-1-56052-190-2

CRISP PUBLICATIONS

INTRODUCTION TO THE SERIES

This series of books is intended to inform and assist those of you who are in the beginning stages of starting a new small business venture or who are considering such an undertaking.

It is because you are confident of your abilities that you are taking this step. These books will provide additional information and support along the way.

Not every new business will succeed. The more information you have about budgeting, cash flow management, accounts receivable, and marketing and employee management, the better prepared you will be for the inevitable pitfalls.

A unique feature of the Crisp Small Business & Entrepreneurship Series is the personal involvement exercises, which give you many opportunities to apply immediately to your own business the concepts presented.

In each book in the series, these exercises take the form of "Your Turn," a checklist to confirm your understanding of the concept just presented, and "Ask Yourself," a series of chapter-ending questions designed to evaluate your overall understanding or commitment.

In addition, numerous case studies are included, and each book is cross-referenced to others in the series and to other publications.

BOOKS IN THE SERIES

DEDICATION

This book is dedicated
to the one I love,
my husband, Myron.

ACKNOWLEDGMENTS

A special thanks to my publisher, Phil Gerould, whose patience is greatly appreciated.

Thank you to all the franchisors and franchisees who shared information that will help others launch a successful business.

CONTENTS

CONTENTS (continued)

CONTENTS

TO THE READERS

Franchises and franchised products are a way of life today. We see them on street corners, signs, trucks, store fronts and even in our homes. This book is about the dream of owning your own franchise. Before deciding on franchise ownership, you need to take a close look at your true interests, skills and abilities. You also need to review and assess your financial situation and long-term goals.

In the following pages, we'll review the benefits of self-employment. We'll show you what to look for in a franchise agreement and what to expect in terms of programs, support and assistance from the franchisor. You'll learn how to check franchisors' earnings claims, how to prepare profit projections for your own potential business, and what to review with your accountant and lawyer before signing any contracts. And, since your own investigation of franchises will be necessary, we'll give you some categories of franchise opportunities to consider.

The world of franchising can be complex and confusing. There are many considerations involved in choosing the franchise that will work for you. To pursue your dream of owning a franchise, keep on reading. This book will guide you in making the best choices for your situation.

Rebecca Luhn

PREFACE

*"Don't set compensation as a goal. Find work you like,
and the compensation will follow."*

—Harding Lawrence

There are basically two types of franchising. An older and less common method is "Product and Trade Name Franchising." Today's method is referred to as "Business Format Franchising."

Product and Trade Name Franchising is an independent sales agreement between supplier and dealer in which the dealer takes on some of the identity of the supplier.

We will concentrate on *Business Format Franchising* in this book. Business Format Franchising is simply an ongoing relationship between franchisor and franchisee that includes a product line, trademarks, service, business strategy, marketing, operating standards, training, and quality control. A long list of businesses fall into this category; i.e., McDonald's, Manpower, Inc., Aamco Transmission, Inc.

A definition offered by the Franchise Consultants Association is as follows:

"A business format franchise is a contractual license granted by one person (the franchisor) to another (the franchisee) which during the period of the franchise:

A. Requires the franchisee to carry on a particular business under a business format or according to a system established by the franchisor

B. Permits the franchisee to use in a connection with such business the franchisor's trade name, trademark, service mark, goodwill and/or know-how

C. Entitles the franchisor to exercise continuing control over the manner in which the franchisee carries on the business which is the subject of the franchise

D. Obliges the franchisor to provide the franchisee with training in the operation of the franchisor's format and/or system, continuing assistance and support in carrying on the business, which is the subject of the franchise (including, but not limited to, assistance with the establishment of the franchisee's business, the training staff, advertising, management and organization of the franchisee's business)

E. Requires the franchisee to make a significant investment from his own resources in the establishment of his own business

F. Requires the franchisee to pay to the franchisor sums of money in consideration for the franchise and/or for goods and/or service provided by the franchisor to the franchisee."

You can find a simpler definition in your dictionary, but basically, franchising is a method of doing business, and it can be used to distribute just about any service or product.

Let's take a closer look at what we'll be covering.

CHAPTER ONE

YOUR PERSONAL CHOICE:

A Self-Assessment

FRANCHIS-ING—THE BEGINNING

"There are always opportunities through which businessmen can profit handsomely if they will only recognize and seize them. . ."

—J. Paul Getty

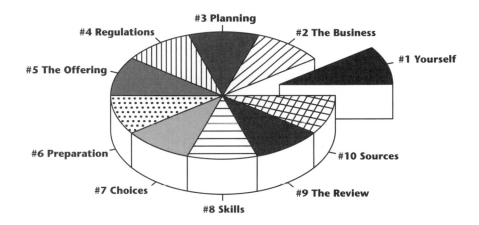

Franchising can be confusing. When choosing a franchise to buy, you may feel overwhelmed in the investigative stages. This book will make the process easier by guiding you through your investigation and by keeping you organized as you compile your research. As in any new venture, we recommend that you thoroughly analyze your objectives and research the background of the business you choose to enter. When your buying decision is based on sound evaluation and thorough research, the franchising opportunity you decide on will make good sense both financially and personally.

The first part of this book will help you understand the business of franchising. It will also help you understand yourself. You'll take a step-by-step evaluation of your goals and the types of business in which you have an interest. Although you'll work with guidelines, you'll be able to determine your own needs and objectives.

The franchise you make a commitment to will be one of the biggest investments in your life. It will also be an enormous legal commitment, and will require a great deal of time and energy on your part.

As you work through this guide, you'll discover most of what you'll need to know about:

- ► Yourself and your business goals
- ► Franchise opportunities
- ► Products and market
- ► Franchise financing
- ► Franchise contracts
- ► Franchise support
- ► Franchise terms

We will work through the following steps:

- ► Taking a close look at your financial capabilities, goals, weak points and strong points.
- ► Examining the potential products or services you have an interest in marketing.
- ► Investigating franchisors and programs that best fit your capabilities.
- ► Working with outside groups and finding additional sources of information.
- ► Submitting franchise applications to companies you have chosen.
- ► Obtaining detailed information on the franchise of your choice and all available legal and financial particulars.
- ► Verifying franchisors' claims of profit and their earnings claims.
- ► Interviewing the franchisees of your choice and verifying good and bad claims.

- ► Interviewing the corporate decision makers of the company you choose and asking all of your important questions.

- ► Having a lawyer review your agreement and negotiate more favorable terms if needed.

- ► Developing a plan of your own and investigating financing.

 **Your Turn**   *Take some time to think about your true career goals and talk them over with your family.*

UNDERSTAND YOUR INTEREST AND ABILITIES

Before you begin your quest of franchisors, you should know your abilities, interests, weak points and strong points. You should also know your financial abilities, goals and restrictions. Self-analysis must be a vital part of the total franchising decision. Taking the time to analyze yourself along with each franchisor will be well worth the effort. Success in any business requires more than a positive attitude, more than hard work and more than sacrifice. You must do your homework, be honest with yourself and have realistic expectations and financial goals.

EXAMPLE

The Case of "Silent for Too Long"

Jane, a thirty-two year old executive for a large mobile phone corporation, had spent four years working day and night to reach the position of sales manager. She was good at her job and knew her product better than most at the top of the organization. Jane had one small problem: she wasn't happy. She told herself over and over that she should be. She was well compensated for someone with her years of experience and the customers liked her. She had a company car and a great benefits package, but something was wrong.

Jane had attended the best schools. Her mother was a lawyer and her father the president of a large computer firm. Jane earned an MBA with honors. Her family was proud of her and told her often how pleased they were with her career.

She was quite good at her finances and had saved for years. So what was the problem? Well, Jane had simply remained silent for too long. She had a passion for two things: she loved her independence and she loved pets. Almost weekly Jane would stop in at the pet shop in her neighborhood. She loved it there. Each time she left, she wished the store were hers. But Jane felt that her parents expected more of her and that she'd disappoint them if she mentioned her desire to own a pet store.

After a long talk with her husband, Jane purchased a small franchise which catered to the needs of pets.

Today, she has three more pet store units from that franchisor and loves her job. By the way, Jane's parents are still proud of her.

Your Turn

Answer these questions:

- ► Will my franchise become my career?

- ► Can I give most of my time to my franchise?

- ► Will I operate and work the franchise myself?

- ► Do I really want to own a business?

- ► Do I really know what it is like to be self-employed?

- ► Do I have the energy to run my own business?

- ► Would I resent giving most of myself to my business in the early years?

- ► Am I truly a hard worker?

- ► Will I give up vacation time to run my business when needed?

- ► Do I have the physical and emotional strength to give to my own business?

- ► Will my family mind the long hours and time away from home? Will they work with me and support the investment?

- ▶ Will the money to finance my new business be a problem?

- ▶ Do I have finances to keep myself going the first year or so of operations?

- ▶ Can I live with the ups and downs of the small business beginnings?

- ▶ Will I miss a regular paycheck?

- ▶ Am I doing this to get rich quick?

- ▶ Am I a risk taker?

- ▶ Will I miss the security of an eight-to-five job?

- ▶ Can I make decisions for myself and others?

- ▶ Am I self-motivated?

- ▶ Am I willing to accept responsibility for the operations and activity of my business?

- ▶ Do I know enough about business management to run a business?

- ▶ Am I organized and can I handle details?

- ▶ Can I supervise others?

- ▶ Can I interview and hire employees?

- ▶ Do I enjoy working with a team?

- ▶ Can I work with the public if needed?

- ▶ Do I know how to promote my ideas?

- ▶ Can I follow the system designed by the franchisor?

- ▶ Can I follow guidelines and work well with others' instructions?

- ▶ Do I respect authority?

- ▶ Can I accept help and take advice?

- ► What am I best at?

- ► Do I want my hobbies and interests to fit into my business?

- ► Do I need more education to do what I want with a new business?

- ► What can't or won't I do?

- ► What are my weaknesses?

- ► What are my dislikes?

These questions are just to start you thinking, but if you can answer them honestly and make yourself a list to use as a guide, you will be well on your way to taking all the necessary steps toward your business decision.

As you work through the chapters in this book you may want to tailor the guidelines to fit your personal situation. We all have different goals, and businesses have their own unique characteristics. You'll find thorough self-evaluations in each chapter.

Take a close look at both your emotional readiness and your physical assets. Franchising is an adventure and should not be taken lightly. The decision to invest in a business may not be entirely rational or based on intellectual consideration. There is always strong emotion that drives our decisions and actions.

Is franchising the right way for you to go into business for yourself? If so, what franchise will be a good match for you? To learn more about the possibilities, we'll take a quick look at the people who buy franchises and some interesting facts from a study group at a university that interviewed business owners and franchise organizations.

Who Buys Franchises?

Those who make the investment and become franchise owners are most likely to:

- Be male
- Be married
- Have a yearly family income of at least $50,000
- Have at least five years of management experience
- Have previously been self-employed
- Desire independence and financial security
- Have had a dream of owning an established business

This casual study shows us that most people who purchase franchises are looking for independence, a desire to be self-employed and the opportunity to make a living with their own expression and drive. *Is this your profile?*

It has also been noted that many who become franchisees make less money during the first few years than they did when they were employed by other companies. But for most new owners of franchises, the psychological rewards outweigh their old paychecks.

Some franchises are purchased as investments by "absentee" owners, or they hire managers and visit the location once or twice a week. Most who are in business for themselves are following a dream of financial security and working independence. Those who follow through with a franchise investment expect a great deal from themselves and want more from life than what they see as the drudgery of a nine-to-five job. They are often risk takers with leadership skills and high ambition. Money is often the number one motivator for America's franchise owners. Additionally, franchise owners have a positive drive and high self-esteem with confidence in themselves and their ability to make business decisions.

Some who desire success buy a franchise because of the image of the company they are buying into and the added experience, expertise, training and guidance they will obtain from the franchisor. Many who have tried to start a business from the ground up recognize their own limitations and know that the reputation and skill provided by a franchisor is often worth the fee. Years of industry knowledge provided in advertising, accounting and basic plans come with most franchise purchases.

It is also known that people who buy a franchise are looking for a business of lasting value. Most franchise agreements are for ten years (we'll explain more in upcoming chapters), but independent businesses are often lucky to make it past their third year.

As you read on, make notes about your own motivating factors. To determine if you are a true candidate for the investment, you'll need to evaluate your mental, physical and financial readiness to continue your quest.

THE TRUTH ABOUT YOURSELF

Ask yourself the following and answer in detail:

1. Have I had a dream of owning a good business and being self-employed, or am I looking for a fast change in my career path? If you have had this dream, write out a description of that dream:

_____

2. Have I always been organized and a good planner? If so, give examples:

_____

3. Do I consider myself flexible and open to change? If yes, in what ways?

_____

4. Do I work well with others, enjoy new ideas and a new environment? If so, give examples:

_____

5. Can I handle stress and the extra pressure that may come with starting a new business?

_____

6. Can I handle the financial details of starting a business and the possible financial risks?

_____

7. Do I enjoy working toward a long-term goal and do I have patience?

_____

Now let's take a look at your basic attitude. Circle the correct answer for you.

1. Owners have more problems daily than their employees.

    A. True
    B. False

2. Employees do not work as hard as their bosses.

    A. True
    B. False

3. Your career is the center of your life.

    A. Often
    B. Occasionally
    C. Never

4. You need recognition for a job well done.

    A. Always
    B. Sometimes
    C. It doesn't matter

5. You do more work in less time than most doing the same job.

    A. Yes
    B. No

6. You feel you could run a business better than most.

    A. Often
    B. Sometimes
    C. Never noticed

7. Most of everything in your life is:

    A. Very organized.
    B. Somewhat organized.
    C. I operate the best I can with what I have.

8. You like to see things done:

    A. As close to perfect as possible.
    B. A good job is good enough.
    C. It doesn't matter as long as it gets finished.

9. How much of your savings are you willing to put into a business?

    A. All of it.
    B. Not savings but a loan.
    C. No financial risk.

10. How well do you adapt to change?

    A. I welcome it.
    B. I accept it but it takes time.
    C. I like things to stay the same.

11. How well do you like the public?

    A. I enjoy and welcome new contacts.
    B. I prefer paperwork and little contact with people.
    C. I do not care to associate with people I don't know.

12. How do you think others feel about working with you?

    A. I enjoy them and they seem to get along with me.
    B. I have had a few on-the-job problems with co-workers.
    C. I stay out of the way of others.

13. Do you enjoy doing all the work by yourself?

    A. I work best alone.
    B. I work well alone but will always ask for help when I need it.
    C. I don't care to tackle any project by myself.

14. How do you react when things don't work out?

    A. I don't mind starting over.
    B. I recover but I'm very cautious.
    C. I won't take a risk. I have to know I have at least a 90 percent chance of success.

15. How do you feel about doing the actual work yourself?

    A. I'm a better manager than worker.
    B. I'll avoid any physical work and hire people when I can.
    C. I believe working at your trade gives you the best experience to train others and produce excellent results.

16. Have you ever trained others at what you're best at?

    A. Yes, at least several or more years in my career has been working at teaching my trade to others, even if on a part-time basis.
    B. On occasion if I'm asked to show someone what to do.
    C. Only once or twice.
    D. Never.

17. Have you ever started a profitable business from scratch?

    A. Yes
    B. No

18. Do you want financial security so you can do more with your life?

    A. Yes
    B. No

SCORE YOURSELF:

1. A=2, B=6; **2.** A=6, B=1; **3.** A=6, B=3, C=1; **4.** A=5, B=3, C=1; **5.** A=6, B=3; **6.** A=6, B=3, C=1; **7.** A=5, B=2, C=1; **8.** A=5, B=3; **9.** A=5, B=3, C=1; **10.** A=5, B=3, C=1; **11.** A=5, B=2, C=1; **12.** A=5, B=3, C=1; **13.** A=4, B=6, C=1; **14.** A=5, B=4, C=1; **15.** A=1, B=2, C=6; **16.** A=3, B=2, C=1, D=0; **17.** A=6, B=2; **18.** A=6, B=3

If you scored:

Over 75   You are near-perfect for the best franchise attitude. Your spirit and drive will carry you far. You have a great deal to offer others and you'll be committed from the start. You are on your way to franchise ownership.

60 to 74   You may need some work on your habits before moving forward with a franchise purchase. You will need to select the right kind of franchise for your abilities. One that is well-established with a proven track record will help support you.

Below 60   Take a closer look at your desire to own a franchise. Ask yourself if you're ready for such a commitment. You should be more prepared for hard work, the reality of risk and your desire to be this responsible. If you believe you can do it, then go back and review your weak points, find a way you can change your attitude and ask yourself if more skill and training would be of benefit before you leap.

The Entrepreneur Profile

You may have an excellent attitude and perhaps your score was quite high, but that is not enough to qualify you for being a successful franchise owner. We'll continue your self-evaluation process with more vital information and soul searching. Remember, you can't pass or fail these tests. They are here so you can honestly discover your own ability and the desire to be a franchise owner.

Earlier we mentioned some traits of independent franchise (business) owners and some of the reasons people are driven to the franchise purchase. Now you can have an opportunity to see if you really fit the "entrepreneur profile."

Please circle the answer that best fits your profile.

1. Are you self-motivated?

    A. I often start projects on my own. I'm rarely asked to get things going.

    B. If someone suggests something, I can get the ball rolling.

    C. I rarely do things on my own and I'll put things off if I can.

2. How do you feel about rules and regulations?

    A. I believe that rules work and respect the authority of others.

    B. I don't think I have to follow them.

    C. I rebel against them and will often do the opposite.

3. Do others listen to your advice?

    A. I can get most people to listen and agree.

    B. Some people follow my ideas if I give them a good reason to.

    C. Most people are too independent to listen.

4. Are you active?

    A. I often take charge and start new projects.

    B. I'll do what others suggest.

    C. I'd rather take life easy.

5. Do you stick with a project?

    A. I'll follow through with my commitments.

    B. I often get side-tracked but I'll finish most things I start.

    C. My initial interest is strong but somehow I lose it.

6. How's your health?

    A. I'm very physical and never feel like I need a long vacation.

    B. I have good energy but I like to take it easy several days a week.

    C. I'm tired most of the time and I get sick often.

7. Are you a good promoter?

    A. Most everyone knows what I do and that I'm proud of it.

    B. I talk about things I believe in with those I know well.

    C. I rarely discuss myself or my business.

8. Do you like new opportunities?

    A. I read and study new ways of doing business and know about the latest ventures.

    B. I keep up with the news but rarely look into new ideas for business.

    C. I wait for someone else to suggest something new to try.

9. Do you waste time?

    A. I try my best to schedule activities and keep busy.

    B. Some days I find myself wondering what I've accomplished.

    C. I daydream and let weeks go by without doing too much.

10. Do you waste money?

    A. I try to budget and keep finances under control and it usually works.

    B. I splurge often but keep track of my income and savings.

    C. I make good money but never can save or seem to have enough.

You can see that the "A" answers show that you'll have the greater ability to be a business owner. The "B" answers show that you need improvement but could be a franchise owner under the right conditions. The "C" answers show great weakness in the given areas.

Now that you've taken a couple of self-evaluations, you may know more about yourself than you really wanted to! As we progress through the analysis, you will learn more about your finances, your readiness to get into franchising and your ability to choose the business best suited to your personality. You'll also discover more about your own ability to work through the rules and regulations that go hand-in-hand with buying a franchise. You'll gain more insight into your ability to negotiate your best franchise agreement.

WILL YOU MAKE A CHANGE?

Before we continue, we want to ask a few questions about your finances. Be as honest and accurate with your answers as possible. If you need to do more research, do so before continuing.

1. What is the maximum investment I'm willing to make in any business, including assistance from another source if necessary?

_____

2. Am I willing to take out a loan and put up a personal guarantee if necessary?

_____

3. What type and how much collateral do I have if I should pursue a loan?

_____

4. Would I take on a partner as an investor or would I look for an outside silent investor if I can't come up with the money? If yes, who would I talk to?

_____

5. Am I willing to work only with franchisors who can offer financial assistance?

_____

6. How much money can I invest without feeling like I'm risking everything?

_____

7. Can I put money into a business now and keep my family going even through slow times?

_____

8. Am I willing to give a business time to work, and will I be able to support myself (family) and any unexpected expenses?

_____

9. Can I put together a realistic financial plan and analysis or do I need help?

_____

10. Can I pay my bills now, or am I looking for a quick fix?

_____

You can see that the answers are all up to you—so be honest and look into any problem areas you may recognize in your financial situation.

YOUR PERSONAL FINANCIAL ASSESSMENT

Where are you financially? Use the following form to work out your assessment of your finances. It has been adapted from forms provided by the Houston Community College accounting department. Many of your local colleges offer classes in financial planning and can be helpful in all areas of operating a small business.

Personal Worksheet

Current Balance Sheet

Assets

Bank Accounts	$_____
Stocks—Current Value	_____
Bonds—Current Value	_____
Auto (if paid off)	_____
Home Value	_____
Other Assets	_____
Total	_____

Liabilities

Loans	_____
Charge Accounts	_____
Installment Purchases	_____
Mortgages	_____
Other Liabilities	_____
Total	_____

Now you've finished a quick assessment of the money you spend and how much you need to satisfy your daily obligations. You've also worked on a personal balance sheet. This should give you a good understanding of where you stand financially.

We'll work more on understanding finances and financial obligations in following chapters o this book, but first we'll view some of the pros and cons of getting into a franchise.

ASK YOURSELF

▶ Are you ready to own your own business?

▶ In what way do you think you fit the profile of a potential franchisee?

▶ What kind of business would you have an interest in and why?

▶ Are you set in a way financially that allows you to make a career change?

CHAPTER TWO

THE BUSINESS OF FRANCHISES:
What You Don't Know *Can* Hurt You

FRANCHIS- ING–ADVAN- TAGES AND DISADVAN- TAGES

"Nothing happens by itself . . . It will come your way, once you understand that you have to make it come your way, by your own exertions."

—Ben Stein

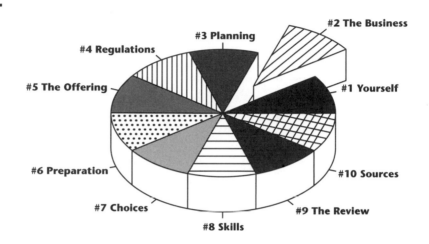

Earlier we gave you a basic definition of a franchise. We'll also give you more approaches to consider, legal considerations and some choices. First, take time to review the advantages and disadvantages of purchasing a franchise.

There are always positive and negative factors associated with any business venture. Some factors are very subjective, others quite objective. Most positive considerations can be reviewed and analyzed on a personal level, but many negatives are major concerns for most who face them.

Advantages

1. A franchise is one way to be an independent business owner.

2. A franchise gives you the opportunity to purchase store merchandise at a discount in large volume.

3. Franchises offer proven training and marketing methods which provide you with the greatest opportunity for success.

4. Most franchises offer solid and defined plans that allow you to start operating as soon as possible. The packages are so complete with materials, rules, operating procedures, advertising and necessary supplies that you are often "off and running" as soon as you open your doors.

5. Highly known franchises are an established method of doing business. A franchise with a known name will draw the public.

6. When your business is a known franchise, the risk of failure is much lower. The established accounting and financial system of a franchise can be of great benefit and the complete training can yield a direct advantage over the independent business operator.

7. If the franchise offers assistance and consultation, it can help you maintain quality and confront serious problems. This can be a great help for some, or an unwelcome hassle for others.

8. The franchisor can offer national and local advertising. This is a wonderful benefit but once again, it won't work for every market. Some franchisors require payment for an advertising percentage. This can be a benefit if it is spent so that the local franchisee receives the exposure. Individual franchise advertising alone can be very expensive. If this can be purchased with the buying power of group purchasing, it can reduce the cost significantly.

9. A good franchisor will stay current on marketing research and product development. This can be expensive for an individual business, but the franchisor can afford to stay on top of the latest in sales and service.

10. If you need a loan to purchase your franchise, you will find that some franchisors have packages that help you obtain financing. They may finance certain parts of the package themselves.

11. The franchisor often has information on the best site selection for the business. This can often be the edge any business needs to get off the ground.

12. There is often an in-depth operations manual that you'll receive with your franchise. This is great for learning techniques that may be unique to that particular type of business.

13. Some franchisors will provide signs, menus, and fixtures, or at least help you procure these items. Others may help with supplies or the purchase of inventory at a discount.

14. You may also receive help with employee hiring, policy and procedures.

These are just a few advantages to look for as you investigate your franchise opportunities. Many advantages will be a matter of your own personal needs, so let's look at some possible disadvantages to franchise programs.

Disadvantages

1. Most successful franchises require a rather substantial investment. You can start most small independent businesses with far less capital. Your franchise may lock you into a contract for several years which could tie up the capital you have invested.

2. Most franchise agreements are several years long, which leaves little room to "try it out" and few options if you don't like your investment.

3. Owning a franchise doesn't provide the same freedom as independent business ownership because the franchise involvement may require you to comply with many rules and regulations.

4. Some franchisors may require that you operate in a particular area which could be high in cost of land or lease space.

5. Some franchisors may require the purchase of certain equipment or that the business look a certain way with a particular type of furnishing. This can be very costly.

6. The advertising percentage fees charged by some franchisors can present problems because the advertising may be used on a national level and be of little benefit to your local area.

7. There may be many restrictions in the franchise agreement. These must be reviewed and considered on an individual level.

8. Few franchisors offer flexibility in their franchise agreement.

These are just a few of the potential advantages and disadvantages to owning a franchise. As you continue to review the ins and outs of the franchise purchase, make your own list of pros and cons. It will be of great benefit to you in your final decision. It is also a good idea to use a pro and con list of each franchise you have a sincere interest in. There may be advantages and disadvantages that are common to all franchise agreements, but there will be many things that differ as you investigate each franchisor.

FRANCHISE PERSPECTIVE

You are just beginning to organize your thoughts about yourself and the franchise business. We touched on some of the main ingredients of a franchise operation as we went through our list of advantages and disadvantages. But there is much more to assess and a great deal more to consider than a simple look at the positive and negative points of franchise ownership.

It is true that you may pay more for a franchise with a solid identity. One of the advantages we talked about in owning an established franchise is the use of the franchisor's registered trademarks, reputation and its local or national recognition. Many people will prefer to pay the larger investment to have the known identity. It is important to note that even a known identity can't guarantee success. There are many other factors that will determine if your franchise will "make it" in the area you select. Success is a blend of marketing, management, product, service location and of course, timing.

OPERATING PROCEDURES

One of the most important ingredients to look for from the franchisor is the level of convenience and comfort with which the franchisor's procedures and operations can be transferred to the new franchisee. When you purchase a franchise, you are receiving more than products and/or the identity of a business. You are also acquiring a particular component that has been proven to work.

Some franchisors will provide you with not only training but business plans, an operations manual, a formula for hiring and proven procedures. You will often receive documents from the franchisor that cover most of the "how-to" procedures relating to accounting and advertising promotions.

Financial Agreements

The more popular franchisors have a three-part fee plan:

1. Payment due when the franchise contract is signed;

2. A royalty or ongoing fee that varies with each franchisor; and,

3. The contribution (usually ongoing) to the local and/or national advertising fund.

If a franchise is not well known and is fairly new in operations, the fees are generally quite a bit smaller. Once the track record is established, the initial buy-in can be considerably higher.

A Short Preview and Checklist

Let's Talk Money and Reputation

- ► What is the initial franchise fee?

- ► Is the fee the same for all locations?

- ► Is there an ongoing royalty fee and is it a percentage of gross revenues?

- ► Is the royalty percentage a set fee or can the franchisor raise it at will?

- ► What are the franchisor's considerations that would cause a royalty charge to be raised?

- ► Is the advertising royalty a set fee and where is it used?

- ► Can there be any other charges by the franchisor over the time of the agreement?

How Well Known

- ► Is the franchise local or national and is it a well-known trade name?

- ► Is there a similar name or business in the area you have an interest in?

- ► Is the image of the franchise a positive one?

- ► Do you want your name associated with this business?

IMAGE ISN'T EVERYTHING

What Does The Franchisor Offer?

► Are signs and furnishings provided or are they extra?

► Does the franchisor help you hire and train employees?

► Are procedures for accounting and record keeping offered?

► How much advertising does the franchisor do and is it in your area?

► Is there help with marketing and sales?

► Is there assistance with technical equipment if needed?

This is the way you should view the franchisor. After all, it is a business opportunity. It consists of a recognized identity, an operating formula, training and ongoing support. Remember, the franchisor is actually selling you a product—the franchise. And like anything else, the better known and better proven product will have the higher price.

Many independently owned businesses do not last long for one reason or another. Much time is spent trying to survive and compete with larger operations. In the world of franchises, a great deal of the trial-and-error period is bypassed. The franchise name and past exposure is certainly an edge but once again, the initial investment is more than likely greater depending upon the industry. We do have a tendency to patronize those establishments with which we are familiar. However, entering into a franchise agreement does not mean quick profits for all. In evaluating a franchise, do not disregard warning lights, or fail to completely examine every aspect and word of the contract.

Being a franchisee is more often than not extremely hard work and can be quite restrictive. Expecting to give too little and wanting too much, too soon can often result in the downfall of a franchisee.

FRANCHISE RULES AND DISCLOSURE IN BRIEF

We don't go into the complete disclosure rules here, but you need to be aware that they do exist and you should review them in full at your convenience. We discuss more about disclosures in later chapters, but now you'll receive a crash course on Rule 436.1, the Federal Trade Commission (FTC) rule governing franchise practices.

If you were to review the overall law, you would find that Section Five begins, "Unfair methods of competition in commerce, and unfair or deceptive acts or practices in commerce, are declared unlawful." The Federal Trade Commission can also bring proceedings against anyone who violates an FTC rule.

Although the Federal Trade Commission's disclosure rule provides the basic federal regulations throughout the country, it still allows *state authorities* to provide additional protection to franchisees. Some states allow the use of the Uniform Franchise Offering Circular (UFOC) disclosure format. The FTC allows the use of the UFOC format in lieu of its own disclosure rule since UFOC also provides protection to franchisees. The FTC rule *does* mandate a minimum period of time in which the UFOC must be viewed by a potential franchisee before any contract may be enforced.

The FTC Rule (436.1) actually declares:

> ". . . It is an unfair or deceptive act of practice within the meaning of Section 5 of (the FTC Act) for any franchisor or franchise broker: (a) to fail to furnish any prospective franchisee with the following information accurately, clearly, and concisely stated in a legible written document at the earlier of the 'time for making of disclosures' or the first 'personal meeting.' "

The Rule is quite clear and defines "personal meeting" as . . .

> ". . . A face-to-face meeting between a franchisor or franchise broker (or any agent, representative, or employee thereof) and a prospective franchisee which is held for the purpose of discussing the sale or possible sale of a franchise."

The term "first personal meeting" does not include any phone or written communications.

The term "time for making of disclosures" is defined as:

"... ten (10) business days prior to the earlier of (A) the execution by a prospective franchisee of any franchise agreement or any other agreement imposing a binding legal obligation on such prospective franchisee, about which the franchisor, franchise broker, or any agent, representative, or employee thereof, knows or should know, in connection with the sale or proposed sale of a franchise, or (B) the payment by a prospective franchisee, about which the franchisor, franchise broker or any agent, representative, or employee thereof, knows or should know, of any consideration in connection with the sale or proposed sale of a franchise."

There is also something called a five-day rule. The franchisor must hand over the complete franchise documents that are for signature by the franchisee at least five business days prior to the date the documents are to be signed in full.

More information is available from the Federal Trade Commission, 6th and Pennsylvania Avenue, N.W. Washington, D.C. 20580, telephone: (202) 376-2805.

Regardless of your understanding of legal documents, we recommend you choose a lawyer who is up to date on the legal aspects of franchising. You cannot be too careful with any investment of this magnitude.

We will tell you more about the disclosure document list, but first we'll offer more information on the business of franchises, planning and financing.

Where Are We So Far?

You should now know:

► To review and understand the Federal Trade Commission Act.

► A little about the Uniform Franchise Offering Circular (UFOC).

- ► To check to see if the franchisors you have an interest in have a true and solid identity.

- ► That you don't sign any agreements or give any money without legal counsel.

- ► To write down everything you hear about the potential franchisor.

- ► To review profits and financials of any franchisor that interests you.

- ► To check whether the franchisor has a proven operating system to offer.

- ► Your current financial status and to narrow down the market you'd like to be in.

- ► What industry interests you.

- ► Yourself and your true potential.

- ► A little about franchisor fees.

Your Turn   ***Complete these activities:***

- ► Take some time to visit your local library and review in full the FTC rules.

- ► Write a short letter to the Federal Trade Commission requesting information that would be of benefit to you.

THE REAL COSTS BEHIND FRANCHISES

Let's Get More Involved

The two basic aspects to most every given product in our society are cost and profit. A simple example: a florist buys several bunches of flowers from a grower for one hundred dollars, then sells twenty flower arrangements made with the purchased flowers for four hundred dollars. The florist has "overhead" costs in the amount of one hundred dollars, covering advertising, delivery, etc. So we can say that the florist has made a profit of two hundred dollars.

The point here is that the cost of a franchise is much like that of the florist. The up-front fee is really of no profit to the franchisor. We could say that the initial fee is often to cover cost, and that the ongoing royalty payments is where the profit is received, but this is not true in all cases.

The franchisor divides the value of the business into three components (this is true for most popular franchise operations, but not for all). The structure is generally based on an up-front or *initial* fee, the *ongoing royalty,* and the *"advertising reservoir."* The first component that is valued is the up-front fee. Most franchisors will tell you that this is not a random amount they dream up, but a well thought out fee based on their costs, consisting mostly of recruiting, training and consulting to new franchises, etc. Some states will require that the franchisors disclose exactly how they arrive at the fee. They will generally use the following elements in their factoring:

1. The projected cost of advertising, plans, signs and other materials.

2. The cost of training.

3. The cost of finding prospective franchises.

4. The value of a particular territory.

5. The value of their identity.

The value of identity may seem somewhat subjective, and some value is perceived rather than based on calculated facts. The value of a business name or identity can be perceived but generally demands that it will raise that value. The lower the risk, the higher the price. Many franchisors who have not established a successful track record offer the sweeter deals. As with any product, you can bet you'll pay more for an established and proven business, a known trade name and excellent territory.

Let's look at some examples:

- *Maaco Auto Painting And Body Works* — Initial License Fee: $15,000

- *Captain D's Seafood Restaurants* — Initial License Fee: $10,000

- *Diet Center, Inc.* — Initial License Fee: $12,000 to $24,000

- *Molly Maid, Inc.* — Initial License Fee: $12,900

- *Ben & Jerry's Ice Cream* — Initial License Fee: $15,000

- *McDonald's Corporation* — Initial License Fee: $12,500

NOTE: All fees listed are approximate and may differ from actual amounts.

Before you get too excited and rush out to purchase a franchise, we will show you some total numbers and how they can change dramatically from the initial license fee.

As you already know, the initial fee is not your only cost. In fact, it is usually just a fraction of the total cost for your franchise purchase. But first,

IN BRIEF: A franchise fee of $10,000 can sound good, but be sure to ask for the franchisor's disclosure of a franchisee's estimated *total initial investment* before you proceed.

EXAMPLE

In the Case of "Too Much Dough"

Jimmy should have asked for more information before taking several hundred dollars out of his savings to fly to New York and attend a presentation on franchise opportunities. A friend had told him that the franchise fee for a pizza shop Jimmy wanted to buy was only $10,000; both Jimmy and his friend believed that this was the total cost to get into the business. But during the presentation in New York, Jimmy soon discovered that the total initial investment was closer to $70,000. Much to his disappointment, Jimmy flew home realizing that at this point in his life, he was not ready or able to come up with this much money. No one was dishonest with Jimmy, but he could have saved his time and money by doing some investigative work first.

Definitions You'll Want To Know

Initial License Fee   The money you pay to the franchisor to become a franchisee. This is charged only once.

Royalties   This is the amount paid to the franchisor weekly, monthly, yearly or on some designated schedule to cover the expense of the franchisor. It can be a percentage of gross revenue, a flat fee, or even a production fee.

Advertising Royalties or Fund   The amount paid toward the franchisor's advertising co-op fund. It can be paid weekly, monthly or on any schedule they require. It may be a percentage of gross revenue or a flat fee.

Minimum Cash Required   The minimum amount of liquid assets in cash that the franchisor requires you to have to qualify as one of their franchisees.

Capital Required   An estimated amount of capital that the franchisor states you'll need to buy and start the franchise.

So, let's look again at the true cost of buying a franchise.

McDonald's Corporation
Initial license fee: $12,500
Royalties: 11.5%
Advertising Royalties: 4%
Minimum cash required: $200,000+
Capital required: $400,000+
Financing: None

Obviously, a McDonald's franchise may not be for everyone, but don't despair. There are much more affordable franchises for sale. For example:

Meineke Discount Muffler Shops, Inc.
Initial license fee: $25,000
Royalties: 8%
Advertising royalties: 10%
Minimum cash required: $45,000+
Capital required: $45,000+

Note: The above are samples and actual numbers may vary.

As you can see, the initial fee may not seem like a great deal of money, so you need to check into the total initial investment. According to the Uniform Franchise Offering Circular (UFOC), the total investment cost must be disclosed. The investment figures should show the initial fee, plus additional costs of setting up and opening the site. If there are costs for equipment, inventory, fixtures, decorations, leases, etc., they must be included in the breakdown of the total cost analysis. An established investment breakdown could look like this:

Initial License Fee	$10,000
Equipment	8,000
Inventory	20,000
Legal Fees	800
Leases	6,000
Working Capital	10,000
Total Initial Investment	$54,800

The estimated cost also shows the working capital during the period of time it will take to get established and profitable.

This is an estimate of the total investment for a fictitious franchise. There are other costs and considerations that we'll need to look at more closely.

We've given you an overview on disclosure, the law, the fees and some of the advantages and disadvantages of owning a franchise. Upcoming chapters contain more information on all of these subjects.

UNDERSTANDING THE FRANCHISE SYSTEM

The franchise network is often referred to as the *ultra-structure*. There are different forms of this ultrastructure, but the least complex is where each franchise outlet is accountable to the franchisor. This is called the *satellite system*. Under some forms, you may purchase your franchise directly from the franchisor or through a broker. In the satellite system, there are no sub-franchisors or brokers, just the franchisee and the franchisor. If a broker or subfranchisor is involved, you may end up paying royalties through them: this way, you pay directly to the franchisor.

There are some benefits to operating within the satellite. A *protected territory* may be one. This is where the franchisor can see that no other of the same franchise can be sold in those predefined boundaries. This does not mean that the franchisee is restricted from selling to customers outside these boundaries.

An example of this arrangement would be if you were to purchase a hamburger franchise in a particular location. The protected territory would mean that the franchisor would not sell another one of their hamburger franchises within some designated boundary. You could advertise for business outside of this geographical area and cultivate business anywhere. This is added value because you are not competing with your own product. It is important that the territory be of value and that market research show the value in your chosen area.

The Franchise Market

Before we get into the ins and outs of market research and evaluating a franchise territory, it is important to know something about the available franchise markets.

Retailing

Obviously one of the leaders in the world of franchising is the retail market. This includes:

▶ *Fast Food* — You've seen them everywhere and on most every corner. Yes, the large chains have grown so fast that they are hard to purchase and require large sums of capital. Those who obtained such franchises early or were able to control a particular territory will prosper for years to come. Many opportunities do exist and even the new smaller chains can result in an excellent investment.

▶ *Product Retailing* — This covers a broad range of merchandise. The products can be electronics, home furnishings, cosmetics, clothing, wallpaper, hardware and lighting fixtures, to name a few. New specialty retailing franchises are showing up every day.

▶ *Convenience Stores* — Convenience stores have certainly grown in number over the years. The purpose served is simply that of the convenience of not having to go to the large supermarket for everyday items. Many of these stores are now found associated with a corner gasoline station.

▶ *Other Food Retailing* — Shops of this nature are everywhere. Health food stores, bakeries and donut shops, candy shops, cafes, ice cream and yogurt shops, and many other types of popular products are offered through franchise operations.

▶ *Auto Services and Parts* — In this type of franchise operation, you'll find a full range of services and the sale of different auto parts. There are also a variety of car washes, repair shops and car component stores.

The Personal and Business Markets

▶ *Personal Services* — Franchises in the areas of home improvement, cleaning, maintenance, carpet cleaning, repairs, etc. are a growth industry. There are many additional types of services, including lawn maintenance, landscaping, pool cleaning, and—a popular one today—burglar alarm systems.

▶ *Business Services* — In this category, you'll find many specialized and varied business services. It could be consultants generalizing in management, accounting, bookkeeping, tax preparation and marketing, etc. It is not unusual to see professional services of all kinds franchised. This includes legal, medical, financial and many other businesses that were once independent.

▶ *Rental Services* — You can rent or lease almost anything these days—from cars, trucks, tools, and supplies to movies, etc. It is a very popular category.

► *Educational Services* — This category has expanded in the past several years with the growing need for computer training, fitness training, and professionals who become trainers themselves.

► *Leisure and Recreational Items/Travel* — You'll find travel agencies, tour agencies, entertainment, spas, health & fitness clubs and specialty sporting goods or equipment in this growing list of franchise opportunities.

Getting Back to Our Evaluation

We can now talk about how different markets and territories rate. Remember, we said that one factor of the franchise fee is the market value. Let's review some geographical territories and their markets. The following are realistic examples, but rank can change annually. Check with marketing research firms or the Small Business Association for most current and detailed market analysis.

► **Food and Beverage Franchise Markets**
Most active areas: Los Angeles; New York; Chicago; San Francisco; Boston; Houston; Dallas; Detroit

► **Retail Franchise Markets**
Most active areas: Los Angeles; New York; Chicago; Boston; Detroit; Houston; Washington, D.C.; Dallas

► **Electronics Franchise Markets**
Most active areas: New York; Los Angeles; Chicago; Houston; Philadelphia; Washington, D.C.; Boston; Dallas

► **Clothing Franchise Markets**
Most active areas: New York; Los Angeles; San Francisco; Houston; Dallas; Washington, D.C.; Boston

As you can see, the most active areas listed rank high in all markets. This does not mean that other cities are not good risks. These are simply the larger and more active marketing areas.

In the past few pages, you've learned a little about the business of franchising. The subjects we covered are expanded upon in upcoming chapters.

Use the following checklist to guide you in your investigation questions. There are more detailed evaluation forms to use once you get into serious negotiations with a franchisor. But even if you're working with a franchise broker, you'll want to make sure that you have satisfying answers to the following questions.

Questions and Answers, A Checklist:

About the initial fee and royalties, you'll want to ask:

1. What is the investment of the initial franchise fee?

2. What does each part of the fee represent?

3. Is there a price for goodwill?

4. Is the franchise well known? And how established is it?

5. Is there any territory represented in the price of the initial fee?

6. How is the territory value compared to other area franchises?

7. What is valued in the initial fee?
   - ❏ Recruiting?
   - ❏ Training?
   - ❏ Operating assistance?
   - ❏ Aids?
   - ❏ Administration?
   - ❏ Manuals?
   - ❏ Advertising?

8. How does the fee compare to that of similar franchise operations?

9. Is the royalty fee reasonable and how does it compare to other similar franchises?

10. Is the royalty fee applied toward advertising or is there an additional co-op advertising royalty charged?

11. How much advertising will I have to do on my own?

12. What is the total cost the franchisor spends on advertising each year? How much of that will be in my chosen area?

13. How are the ads run and what media are selected?

14. How much assistance will I receive from the franchisor?

15. How vast is the territory of the franchise of my choice?

16. Is the market good for the type of franchise I'm considering?

These are just a few of the questions you'll begin with as you look into franchise fees, territory and royalties. We'll find out later just what a franchisor will do to get your attention and commitment!

ASK YOURSELF

► What are the pros and cons of buying a franchise?

► Are you willing to take the time to investigate any franchise opportunity that interests you?

► What are the documents the franchisor is required to provide?

CHAPTER THREE

PLANNING, FINANCES AND FINANCING: From Start to Finish

THE PRICE OF DREAMS

"An intelligent plan is the first step to success, the man who plans knows where he is going, knows what progress he is making and has a pretty good idea of when he will arrive."

—Basil S. Walsh

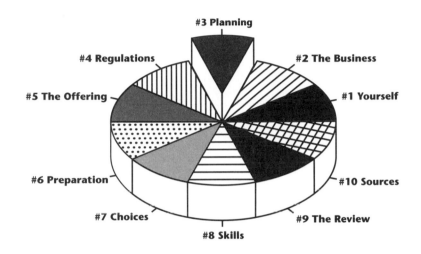

Money, Money, Money!

Yes. It all takes money. Franchising can have some rather large returns but as you can see, it often takes money to make more money.

You may be asking yourself where it will come from!

We mentioned briefly that some franchise operations offer financing. For those looking for financing elsewhere, we'll briefly discuss some options.

In order to obtain any type of financing, you will need to prepare a business plan that demonstrates how much financing is needed and how it will be used. It assures the lender that the loan will be repaid in a reasonable amount of time. A business plan also includes an analysis of earnings potential. This is useful if you ever plan to obtain additional capital from outside investors. Before we go into a brief description of the types of financing, we are going to discuss the contents of a good solid business plan.

THE PLAN

The most common business plans contain the following:

- A business concept
- Market considerations
- Management
- Financial performance
- Payback analysis

An Overview of What to Include

▶ **The Business Concept**
This section of the plan states the type of business, the products or services involved and the customer base. This is where you discuss in detail the franchise operation you've selected and its formula for success. This opening should "hook" your reader and have strong concrete statements supported by facts and figures. It is important to show the dynamics of the operation and the earnings for such an industry.

▶ **Marketing Considerations**
This section shows your plan to market the products or services. It should include a customer profile, advertising strategies, and analysis of the market as a whole. You can also include statistics on past advertising campaign payoffs. You'll obtain most of this information from the franchisor.

▶ **Management**
This shows your qualifications to run the operation and your credentials. You'll outline your role, responsibilities and past successes.

► **Financial Performance**
This section provides projections of future performance. These are based and backed by the pro-forma operating statements of the franchise operation itself and include at least three years of projected income and expenses. The franchisor's own financial forecast statements are helpful here.

► **The Payback Analysis**
The return is based on the present value of the investment and what will be an attractive return on that investment. Here you show case histories (they can be provided by the franchisor) on actual returns.

To obtain start-up financing or additional capital, you'll want to include the following information:

A. The basic information about the franchise itself, including services and/or products.

B. Information about yourself and any partners who will be directly involved in the business.

C. The amount of financing needed.

D. Where and how the proceeds will be distributed and utilized.

E. Research about the target market.

F. Customer profiles.

G. Past and projected earnings.

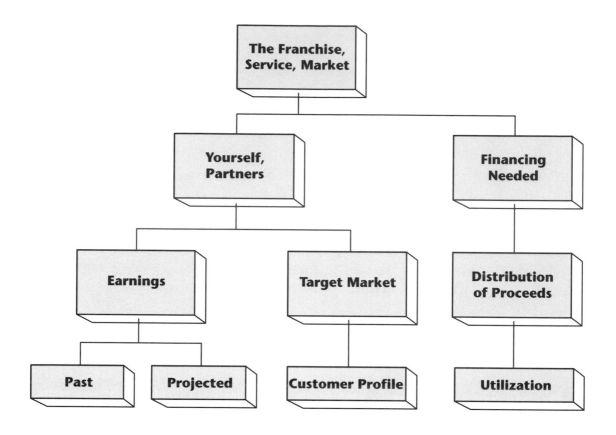

You will find that a great deal of the information you need can be provided by the franchisor. A well-developed franchisor will have packaged information on products, marketing, earnings, expenses, etc. Established franchisors will have statements on the past earnings of operations in a similar area. This information will be an advantage when looking for capital.

Easy to Obtain?

They'll want to know . . .

► **About the Franchise**
This is in your franchisor's disclosure statement. It is best to condense the franchisor's version because many are quite lengthy. If you summarize the information on the company, the history and its products,

you will offer enough information to satisfy most, but you should offer the entire statement and make it available upon request. Once you are ready to obtain financing to expand an existing operation of a franchise, you'll need to include information on your own operations.

► Your Working and Non-working Team

Don't forget to include information about your partners, working or silent, and any members of your management team. Every financial source will be interested in any and all key players. The financing source is obviously lending money with belief that with success, they will be repaid. A strength in that consideration is management. An in-depth résumé of yourself and staff is of significance with strong emphasis on management experience. You'll increase your chance of acquiring financing if you include personal information about yourself and your staff along with backgrounds of any accountant or attorney you'll employ. Lenders also have a strong interest in the planned structure of your organization.

► How Much and What Kind of Money

You'll need to request the type of financing you'll require and the amount along with information on the terms. Several types of financing can be requested and this is not considered unusual. Types may include an intermediate-term loan, a line of credit or even secured notes. You should also provide a schedule of how much you'll need at different stages.

► Your Intent

You'll want to explain how you'll use each type of loan that you request. For example, if you request an intermediate-type loan, you may indicate that it will be used to purchase the needed operating equipment. A line of credit may be needed to keep inventory stocked.

► More on Marketing

You'll get the basic marketing information from your franchisor but the lending source will certainly want more. They'll want information about the area you'll be operating in and the demographics. You'll need to include local advertising and promotional information. The plan should show the size of your sales team, target accounts and any area competition. Of course, how much and what information you provide in this area will depend upon the type of franchise operation you want to own. Under this part of the plan, your study should show not only a type of target account, but a complete profile of the customer you'll expect to target.

THE IMPORTANCE OF FINANCIAL STATUS

A lender may be impressed with all you've provided up until this point, but if your financial information is not detailed and convincing, you may not qualify for a loan. Their consideration is based on whether or not they believe you can make a profit and repay the loan.

► Personal finances are just that. The lender will want a list and value of each asset, liquid asset, cash, etc. They'll also want to know what you already owe, a complete list of liabilities and the terms you have agreed to for repaying any loans you already have.

► The operating statement will be based on your researched projections and includes estimates of income and expenses for one to three years. You may have to do some serious projections since you'll probably only be looking at your budget one year at a time. Be careful not to get carried away here. A lender will want realistic projections, not "pie in the sky" figures. You can obtain some helpful numbers from the franchisor who has information about franchisees in a similar market area within the same franchise. This will help validate your estimates and justify the market area you'll be operating in. If there is demonstrated success from a similar demographic study, there is a good chance you'll have success in the eyes of the lender.

Some lenders may also ask for first, second and third-year balance sheets from similar franchise units within the franchise operation. Some may want cash flow projections on a month-to-month basis.

Even if not required by the lender, you'll still want to complete your break-even point. This is the intersection of the total-sales and the total-costs lines. Above that point, the company begins to make a profit, but below that point, it demonstrates a loss. This analysis is a mathematical technique for analyzing the relationship between profits and variable costs. It is also a good profit-planning tool for calculating the point at which sales will equal total sales.

What You Don't Know Can Hurt You

Understanding Financial Statements. It is all too common that we ask others for explanations of our financial statements. Balance sheets and operating statements are typical reports needed for franchise operations. Without a clear understanding of these figures, a franchisee (or even potential franchisee) can be misled as to the worth or value of the franchise and may not clearly see the profit or loss figures. Hiring professionals is certainly an important asset to any business, but even if you ask your accountant for explanations, it is best that you learn and understand all statements yourself.

Operating Statements. Often referred to as profit and loss statements, these statements of income reflect both expenses and income for periods of time; a month, quarter or a year. They reflect the following and you should know how they are figured.

▶ Cash and credit sales for the period of time adjusted for sales tax receipts. Often a franchisor's royalties are based on total sales, so it is important to show all transactions.

▶ To compute the cost of goods that have been sold, you'll add your purchases made to your starting inventory, then subtract the total from your ending inventory.

▶ Your next line will show gross margin, sometimes called gross profit. You'll subtract the cost of goods sold from your sales to obtain these figures (Net Sales – Cost of Goods Sold).

▶ If there is income from anything other than sales, you'll include that at this point on the operating statement.

▶ All selling expenses will then be included. You'll show payroll, franchise royalties, advertising, etc. All expense categories must coincide with budget categories for the same period of time. If you as the owner of the franchise draw a salary, you should show it here. If you own and operate more than one franchise unit, you may wish to show your compensation and that of other offices under a separate category as part of expenses incurred by "central administration."

▶ Also show all general and administrative expenses. Include employee benefits, insurance, depreciation, etc.

▶ If a corporation, you'll show a category on income tax. Net income before taxes and net income after taxes.

▶ Last but not least, your net profit.

Statements will have greater meaning as you become familiar with them and have more opportunities to review those from the franchisor.

Balance Sheets

In this report, you should know:

▶ Current assets. Shows cash at hand, inventory, any prepaid expenses, accounts receivable, accounts receivable less allowances for doubtful accounts.

▶ Fixed assets. Shows land, building and equipment. Book value of these items that are necessary to operate the franchise will be your total fixed asset number. These numbers are often overvalued because these items are often recorded according to a depreciation schedule and not resale value. This is fine unless a realistic number is needed at the sale of a business or the closing of a business. Remember the true value of something is what someone will pay for it. So if you have something with no or little market value, it doesn't do much good to carry that item on the book with a value close to the original cost.

► Any other assets that are not liquid and related to the franchise are in a separate class. They may consist of loans receivable, investments, insurance with cash value that is payable to the franchise and other related items.

► The next line on the balance sheet often reflects current liabilities. You'll generally list notes payable, accounts payable, accrued payroll, taxes payable, accrued expenses and unearned income, etc. You'll often see unearned income on the asset list, but not as a liability. You'll find few franchises have this problem unless they deal with advance deposits as payments. The liabilities listed are set to be paid at the end of the current fiscal period.

► If you have debt that has a maturity date exceeding 12 months, you have "long-term debt" and the total should be adjusted for the amount listed as a current liability.

► If needed, you'll show any equity and then reconcilement of equity. This will generally be either shareholder's equity or, if a partnership, the partners' equity; sole proprietors will show the amount of capital put into the franchise, profits retained and then subject losses or money withdrawn.

Now that you have a good idea of what to look for in operating statements and balance sheets, it would be helpful to begin a study of definitions you may deal with in the world of finances. The definitions are common, but knowing them will be well worth the effort in your quest for financing.

Common Definitions

Average daily credit sales — are obtained by dividing the credit sales for a period of time by the number of days in that time frame.

Common equity — the common shareholder's investment in the franchise. It is measured by subtracting total debt and preferred stock from total assets. This may be common stock, or even retained earnings accounts.

Contribution margin — the excess of net sales revenue over variable operating costs. It represents the contribution of revenues to the fixed operating expenses and profit.

Current assets — the resources that can be turned into cash within a period of time, usually twelve months.

Current debt — represents all liabilities that are payable in one year or less.

Equity — the ownership interest in the franchise. Usually calculated by subtracting the total of all debt from the total of all assets.

Fixed operating costs — those expenses that remain unchanged for the most part. Overhead requirements generally stay the same as production and sales levels change, unless there is expansion, salaries increase and additional insurance, etc., is required.

Funded debt — represents long-term obligations, such as mortgages, term loans, bonds and other such liabilities maturing one year past the date of the finance.

Gross profit — the net sales minus the cost of the goods sold.

Liquid assets — cash or liquidable assets of the franchise.

Mean — cash assets of the franchise are liquid assets and include highly marketable money market instruments.

Net assets — the total of assets minus current liabilities.

Net sales — shown by subtracting sales returns and allowances and cash discounts taken on sales from the gross sales.

Net working capital — the excess of current assets over current debt. You get this number by subtracting the total current debt from the total current assets.

Operating assets — the assets the franchise needs for its normal daily activities. If you subtract such things as real estate, unrelated securities and intangible assets, and all other non-operating assets from your total assets, you'll have your number for operating assets.

Operating profit — the net of sales minus all the related operating expenses.

Quick assets — total current assets minus the inventory.

Tangible net worth — the owners, stockholders or partners' equity in the franchise. It is derived by subtracting total debt from total assets and then deducting the dollar amount of intangible assets carried by the franchise.

Total debt — the total of current liabilities and long-term liabilities.

Variable operating costs — the expenses which vary with the level of production and sales, such as direct labor and direct material.

Once again, you'll want professionals to review all statements offered by the franchisor, but as you become a franchise owner, you'll be glad you're familiar with all financial statements, for one day you'll prepare your own.

ABOUT YOUR SUMMARY DOCUMENT

Remember that applying for financing is much like submitting a job résumé. There is often an initial review by people other than those responsible for approval of the loan. This is the process of elimination. It is not until the lender has a sincere interest that the complete plan would be looked at in detail. So just as it is important to have a cover letter accompany your job application, it is equally as important to have a summary with your loan application. With this you'll want to attract the attention of the initial screeners and also offer a quick way that they can review your proposal without reading the entire document.

As for most abstracts, it should only be two pages and contain at least the following information:

1. Identify the franchisor and franchise.

2. All parties involved and location.

3. How much financing you'll need.

4. The purpose of the funding.

5. A brief description of the potential customers and the market.

6. Potential profit and your source.

7. Your ability to repay the loan.

It is important that this document be well written, professional and brief. If you are not good at proposals, we urge you to contract professional services so your package will be attractive and effective. As with any request for financing, you stand a better chance for review if you have a contact and if you can get an appointment with the lender for the review in person.

Once you pass the initial review process, you'll move into the next steps: evaluation and confirmation. This is where the lending institution will check and confirm the information you've given them. They'll do a credit check and verify information about the franchisor. They'll take a careful look at financial figures and produce ratios that serve a purpose but are not the sole determination for obtaining the loan. The factors they'll look the closest at will be your history, your experience, abilities to manage and organize and of course, your ability to repay them.

SOURCES OF FINANCING

Where Do You Begin to Look for Financing?

Think about:

- Banks
- Family and friends
- Venture capitalists
- Investment bankers
- Stockbrokers
- Commercial loan companies
- Small Business Administration
- Local development groups
- Corporations
- Credit Unions
- Mutual funds
- Pension funds
- Business agents
- The franchisor

A Closer Look at a Few of the Financial Sources

► **Small Business Administration**

If you have been turned down by three other funding sources, you can qualify for an SBA-guaranteed loan. The loan is actually offered by a bank but if you default, you would be backed by the SBA. The SBA loan guarantees are limited and the guidelines vary, depending on the general classification of the enterprise. There are small business lending companies that are licensed by the SBA. They lend to franchisors for start-up but don't offer lending to franchisees.

► **Commercial Banks**

The banking industry is ever-changing and few are making loans for business start-ups. The smaller independent banks are much more open to the idea of extending the loans for small business and some are involved in the Small Business Administration loan guarantee program.

► From the Franchisor

Very few franchisors will give direct financing today. Many will offer assistance in finding a lender and some have lease programs. When you contact the franchisor, they'll be able to give you information on assistance they offer.

► Venture Capitalists

Venture capitalists have always been a source of money needed for the larger businesses. This is not often a favorite for the small franchise because of the extremely high return they request on their investment, and they often want equity in the operation.

► Individual Investors

Yes, there are those who search for a place to invest money. They are usually diverse and offer short-term notes with arrangements set up through brokers. Some are looking for partnerships and are willing to give more for a larger and greater return. Check out the reputation of possible investors and learn to understand the terms completely.

BUSINESS AND PLANNING WORKSHEETS

The following worksheets will help you put your thoughts on paper and outline the information you need to prepare for your final proposal. *They should be used as a guide only.* Your final proposal and plan should be completely detailed and professional.

Briefly describe what you'll put down for each topic or at least note where you'll obtain the information.

Cover Sheet _____

Work Goals _____

Your Personal Information _____

I. The Franchise and Its Business

    A. Describe the Franchise _____

       _____

    B. Describe the Products and Services _____

       _____

    C. Location of the Franchise _____

       _____

    D. The Franchisor and Its History _____

       _____

    E. You and Your Team _____

       _____

II. The Marketing Plan

    A. Target Customers _____

    B. Demographics of Market (who are your buyers and what are they like?)

       _____

       _____

    C. How Does Your Franchise Compare to Others? _____

       1. Price Comparison _____

       2. Quality Comparison _____

III. Financial Worksheets

A. Possible Sources of Funding _____

_____

B. Capital Needed and For What _____

_____

C. Balance Sheet _____

_____

D. Break-even Analysis _____

_____

E. Income Projections (Profit and Loss Statements) for Franchise

    1. Three-year Summary Projection
    2. First Year
    3. Second and Third Years

F. Pro-Forma Cash Flow

    1. First Year
    2. Second and Third Years

Your Turn   *Complete this activity:*

▶ To learn more about securing the capital you may need a better understanding about preparing financial proposals. Contact a local university or the SBA office in your area and find out about a seminar you can take on the subject.

MORE ABOUT MONEY AND COSTS

Money is often the principal interest for getting into a franchise, but not the only one. It just happens that it can be the reason you stay in business, fail in business or struggle through the business. As we stated earlier, the purchase of the right franchise can be a larger investment initially than if you started a business from scratch, but you do increase your survival chances with a known name and the franchisor's experience.

Why Do Some Franchises Fail?

- Change in public interest
- Loss of capital
- Inexperience in managing a business
- Lack of income
- Not adapting to current market changes

It is important to look closely at the success rate of the franchisees and the franchisor's ability to stay current with the industry.

You must also be realistic about potential earnings in the franchise of your choice. If the earnings are not enough to support your family in the style you need, you will toil hard without much reward. For some franchisees, earning an average income is enough if they have their freedom. For others, the rewards are great, and they can make more money than they ever thought possible. It all takes planning and patience, but most of all, you must know how to manage the money.

Where Will the Money Go?

Let's look at some general expenses most franchise operations have.

1. *Advertising:* We said earlier that there can be a flat fee paid to the franchisor that will go into an advertising pool. You may also spend a great deal on your own local

advertising if it is not provided for by the franchisor. If you do make payments to the franchisor, you'll probably list this fee separately. You may also want to break the advertising amount into a monthly expense because many businesses have greater advertising expenses at different times of the year.

2. *Transportation:* If the business requires the use of automobiles for sales or service, you'll want to include this expense along with insurance licensing fees and interest on such vehicles.

3. *Collection Expenses:* If you offer credit, you'll need to know the real cost to you in terms of extending the credit and collections.

4. *Insurance:* Insurance premiums add up, so be sure to include all related expenses such as general liability, fire, auto, etc.

5. *Salaries and Wages:* You'll generally have a good feel for how much help you'll need because the franchisor will give you an idea of how many employees it should take to keep the operation open. The average staffing can often be adjusted according to your willingness to be hands-on and your family's interest in working the business. Remember that the total costs of compensation can be more than 40 percent of direct salary. Don't forget your own salary!

6. *Professional Services:* It is important to budget for this category. Professional advice can be invaluable as you learn the business.

7. *Rent:* Although a good location is important, don't forget that leasing or renting space can take a large percentage of the budget. Depending on the business you choose and your market research, the amounts will vary.

8. *Office Expense:* Any and all administrative and office expenses not provided by the franchisor will cost you money each month. So look closely at your franchise agreement to see what is covered.

9. *Royalties:* We talked about royalties earlier and the schedules vary depending upon sales. To ensure yourself a safety net, budget for a high rate and the more you sell, the better you'll feel.

10. *Utilities and Other Expenses:* There are several other expenses that may be a concern. Utilities can be one if not included in your lease. It is difficult to budget for this, especially since you won't know an average cost until you've been operating for a few months. Don't forget telephone and other needed daily equipment expenses.

11. *Taxes, Fees and Other:* It is a good idea to check with your accountant on local and state taxes in your area and licensing fees, etc.

Other Expenses (a quick checklist)

- Supplies
- Bank charges
- Travel expenses
- Freight/shipping
- Commissions
- Employee taxes and benefits
- Cost of goods sold

Depending upon the type of franchise you select, there may be other expenses, or many of these may not even be a consideration. Just don't be caught by surprise. Ask the franchisor for estimates!

BEWARE OF POTENTIAL PITFALLS

Common Sense

You've heard the story and you've seen the signs: "Going Out of Business Sale." What causes a great business in an excellent location to fail? Most failures are financially related errors by the owners.

What You Just Don't Know

Once you're into your franchise operation, you should feel confident in running the business and knowing all you need to know. Although the franchisor will often provide you with more than adequate training, you need to be tuned into changes of all kinds.

Changes that can affect your success are:

1. Changes in new products from competitors.

2. Changes in technology.

3. Changes in the economy.

4. Changes in customer attitudes.

5. Changes in buying trends.

6. Changes in your territory.

Being aware of your surroundings and staying on top of the market is an excellent offense. Leaving your success up to your franchisor is not advisable. Be sensitive to their attitude toward change and don't hesitate to question their past activity and ability to keep you with the times.

Don't Begin with a Struggle

Inadequate working capital can cause any business to fail. Having enough capital at the start and keeping adequate working capital is obviously very important. If you start with enough but develop a shortage, you have options:

1. *Add capital yourself.* If you feel good about the business and you realize adding capital will bring success, then do so. You can use your own assets or again put up your assets as collateral for a loan. Sometimes a small infusion is all it takes but be practical about your choice.

2. *More sales.* Sounds good to most everyone, but oftentimes an owner expects the franchise to speak for itself, or they put the focus on operations and not sales.

3. *Cut back on the business.* Seems to go against the grain, but it can be a band-aid to keep things comfortable. This is often a temporary solution, but downsizing has become a common practice for businesses both small and large. It allows for the business to operate in its most profitable areas and produce the cash flow.

4. *Better management.* Attention to details and better cash management can make the working capital you have provide a more productive level of business. Pay attention to receivables and inventory levels and you'll often find that your money goes further and works better for you.

5. *Find a lender.* If you know your franchise is going in the right direction, but needs a little support to move forward faster, you can attract lenders or investors. Be sure to check the terms and make sure the conditions will be best for the business in the long run.

Don't Overextend

It is true that many franchise owners get into financial trouble because they overextend in facilities, equipment or property. It is possible to sell the excess assets and lease any necessary equipment or property. This provides more immediate and usable funds. This option is available if the franchise agreement will allow it.

Excess

Too much spending can damage the working capital and break the business if not managed. There is only one way to handle this, and that is to cut back. Reduce perks, cut back on unnecessary expenses and cut back salaries if necessary.

Keep an Eye on Inventory

Rule of thumb is to beware of keeping inventory low. This can result in loss of sales and customer dissatisfaction. Too much inventory can result in getting stuck with obsolete items. Knowing when and what to buy is important. The track record of other franchises (obtained from the franchisor) can help. Find out about volume purchases but first be sure you can move your inventory. If you deal with seasonal products, move your products at the end of the season with promotions or sales. Proper inventory and proper pricing can make a significant difference in profit or loss. Again, check your agreement for any restrictions.

Expanding Too Soon

The temptation to expand can be a downfall. You must give careful consideration to expansion. Bigger isn't always better. Make sure what you have is working before you branch out. When you're ready and the research is complete, you'll know if the time is right. Until then, keep a close watch on what you have.

Careful with Compensation

It is often easy for the owner and any working family to take out more for themselves than the franchise can really afford. There must be controls on compensation, sound budgets and projections.

Collection Is Never Easy

If you provide credit to customers, be advised that there will come a time when it may be difficult to collect. In fact, you are lending money out when you wait to be paid for your products or services. Your credit system should be simple and efficient and you should have a sound policy for collections. Have a working knowledge of today's credit and collection laws. These are not provided by the franchisor. In brief, the Uniform Commercial Credit Code allows you certain rights:

► You have the right to contact and verify employment if a person signs a credit application.

► You have the right to check references.

► You can retain a credit bureau to check for you.

- ▶ If a buyer defaults, you can demand payment or repossess the merchandise.

- ▶ You can sue for moneys owed to you.

- ▶ You can require payment even if the purchase is offered back to you once a purchaser is delinquent—and you do not have to accept the return.

- ▶ You do not have to accept partial payment if you obtain a judgment.

These are just a few of your rights. You have additional rights, so learn them and act within the law.

You may have decided by now that you'll need help with all of this, so . . .

Who Ya Gonna Call?

Working with and Choosing the Right Professionals

We advise that you seek out qualified professionals who can help you in every area. This is extremely important even if you're familiar with financial documents.

We advise that you work with the following:

1. *An accountant.* In review and for basic computations for cash flow of the franchisor's financial statement, an accountant can provide you with information that may not be clear from the paperwork alone.

2. *An attorney.* The nature of franchise documents puts them in the category of needing legal advice. It is important to have an attorney evaluate the franchise offering circular, agreement and other documents. An attorney should be completely knowledgeable in franchise law and have experience with franchise arrangements. It is important to locate and contract an attorney who works for the franchise as well as the franchisor. This point is important in the evaluation process.

Where Are We?

You should have a good idea at this point for the workings of a franchise business. Now we'd like to review in more detail the laws affecting franchising and the importance of completely understanding the franchise agreement.

While reviewing this chapter, remember that in order to obtain start-up money, you need a good proposal. As we stated, the franchisor will provide much of your needed information, but be sure your proposal is complete. Include your résumé, personal financial statement and all franchisor information. Above all, remain optimistic!

We worked through understanding a great deal about the finances and their working relationship to the franchise, franchisor and the franchisee.

It is equally important to obtain and understand as much as you can about the legal issues surrounding the world of franchises. In addition, it will be paramount that you read and analyze all documents you receive from the franchisor. When it comes to the franchise contract, what you don't know *can* hurt you. So we do advise that you work closely with professionals and familiarize yourself with all documents before entering into any negotiations.

In the next chapter, you'll have a chance to examine more closely what to look for and what to expect. When you finish your review of that valuable information, study the sample documents so you'll know what to expect.

ASK YOURSELF

▶ What is so important about having a plan?

▶ What are the elements of a standard business plan?

▶ Where will you receive much of the needed information for a financial proposal based on the franchise interest you are pursuing?

UNDERSTANDING FRANCHISE REGULATIONS AND AGREEMENTS:
You Can't Know Too Much

IMPORTANT INFORMATION AND MORE

"There is no road too long to the man who advances deliberately and without undue haste; there are no honors too distant to the man who prepares himself for them with patience."

—Jean De La Bruyere

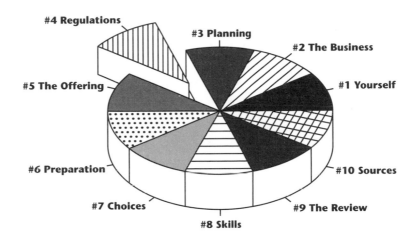

In a later chapter, we provide you with evaluation forms and checklists to use when in front of the franchisor. In this chapter we will review the importance of the checklist and tell you a little more about the reasons behind the questions. We'll also tell you what to look for when you review the disclosure list. And we'll help you understand a franchise agreement.

Take your time as you review the main points of each area. Then review the samples. When you've finished, you will have enough educated and comprehensive questions to take on any franchisor.

So what will you want to know? Let's take a look . . .

Important Points: Questions Often Asked and Questions to Ask

It is important to note that most franchisors will provide you with much of the following information. If not, you'll want to do some research.

1. **Question:** Is it important to know how long the franchise has been in business?

    Answer: If the franchisor has been in business for several years, there should be a solid record. On the other hand, if the business is fairly new and it has only been in operation a few years, it would be difficult to find out much about the business and it is wise at that point to research the history of the owners.

2. **Question:** What kind and types of data should one expect to see from the franchisor?

    Answer: Profit and loss statements are going to be some of the most important sets of figures you'll want to see. It is also important to realize the market you're looking at. Marketing professionals can help here and the figures will certainly have to be interpreted in that light. Many franchisors are hesitant to release profit and loss statements if you are only shopping around. You'll have to be insistent in order to get their cooperation. But if you meet with them, you'll find the information in the disclosure documents.

3. **Question:** Is it important to know if the franchisor is making money?

    Answer: Yes, you'll want to know what financial shape the franchisor is in. This is information your accountant can help you with upon a review of their documents. They certainly should show you if the franchisor is making money from the success of franchises and royalty fees generated, or if money is coming in from another source.

4. **Question:** How will one know if a franchisor has a good reputation and rating?

Answer: You'll need to do your homework. Reports from local and national Chambers of Commerce, Dun and Bradstreet, Better Business Bureau, and bankers, etc. and information listed in the franchisor's history can all help with obtaining the facts.

5. **Question:** Does it help to interview current franchisees of the franchisor?

   Answer: Yes, it is very important to call both new and older franchisees of the company. The newer franchisees will give fresh information on how helpful the franchisor has been in the start-up, but we caution you that they'll also be very dependent on the franchisor early on. They also may not know enough to give a fair report. Your interview checklist in this book will help guide you. A franchise that has been operating for some time will have more useful information but be careful to confirm all negative comments.

6. **Question:** What does one look for when reviewing success and failure rates among the franchisees?

   Answer: When reviewing the failure rate, you want to know the number of franchisees terminated, not the number sold from one franchisee to another. It is more important to discover the amount of money lost in terminations than it is to accept a 90 percent success claim.

7. **Question:** If a franchisor has many franchises operating, does this indicate a better track record?

   Answer: You'll need to look at the history. Review the numbers from previous years, this year and the projected numbers. As you do your analysis, you can use these figures to compare several different franchisors.

8. **Question:** What else should we know about the product or service the franchise offers?

   Answer: This is a good time to check with marketing professionals and obtain consumer information. Other operating franchisees can give insight into the acceptance of the product or service. The length of time it has been around is also important. Ask: Is it here to stay or is it a fad?

9. **Question:** Is it important to compare different franchisor contracts?

   Answer: Yes, evaluate and compare related contracts. This will help you determine if the fee is justified or if a higher fee can generate more services.

10. **Question:** Will royalty payments vary among different franchisors?

    Answer: You'll find varied percentages among franchisors. Make sure your comparison is with like operations. Often the percentage of gross sales or the royalty percentages will depend upon the length of time in business. Obviously, the larger chains with high visibility and a solid reputation will charge more.

11. **Question:** How will one determine how much money will really be needed?

    Answer: You'll have to do a great deal of investigating. Franchisors often suggest numbers lower than the amount you'll end up needing. Use a form to calculate all projected total investment costs and ask other franchisees how close their real costs were to the numbers given by the franchisor.

12. **Question:** What are the purchasing requirements of most franchisors?

    Answer: Each will have different requirements. Some do not have a minimum purchase in order to maintain the agreement. You'll need to check the agreement closely, compare with others and find out the cost.

13. **Question:** How restrictive are the franchisor's requirements for exclusive operation in their franchise?

    Answer: Some will require that you operate exclusively in their franchise business, many do not. Check the contract and determine if this will hamper you and your future interest if it is one of the restrictions.

14. Question: When would the contract from the franchisor be available?

Answer: You should have access to a specimen contract upon request, but many may request that along with your application you submit your financial documents before they'll release their sample agreement and disclosures.

15. Question: What should be the norm for assistance offered by the franchisor?

Answer: There are no set specifications on just how much assistance a franchisor should offer. But you'll want to ask about their assistance in the following areas:

1. Public relations and advertising.
2. Training and operations manual.
3. Terms for purchasing products.
4. Store layout, displays and equipment.
5. Continuing assistance.
6. Inventory control.
7. Location and territory.

16. Question: Do most franchisors offer protected territory?

Answer: Some do, and others do not. If they do, check the terms and consider the location and what is considered to be fair distance for a particular area. Ask how the franchisor protects this territory and what legal means are the basis of the territory protection.

17. Question: What should we look for in the agreement regarding renewability, termination or ability to sell?

Answer: Check the contract for the length of the franchise agreement and terms for raising fees. Find out if the franchisor can terminate the agreement and if so, under what conditions. The best advice is to let your attorney check the details and note any red flags.

18. Question: Should everything the franchisor promises be in the contract?

Answer: Yes, if it is an important issue, put it in writing.

The questions above are the most common asked by potential franchisees. If you have any, write them down and keep asking until you obtain a satisfactory answer.

Many of the questions we just reviewed will be answered in the offering circular along with the contract. If you should find that provisions you have an interest in are not addressed, you should first meet with an attorney knowledgeable in franchise agreements. Then meet again with the franchisor for additional information. Prior to this meeting, you should have asked the franchisor about elements of the contract that are negotiable.

Now, an in-depth look at the law . . .

More On Regulations

We briefly discussed the laws in earlier chapters of this book, but now we will go over the requirements in greater detail.

As we stated earlier, the Federal Trade Commission (FTC) introduced its "Trade Commission Rules" in 1979, which require all franchisors operating anywhere in the United States to make full disclosure to all prospective franchisees. We also mentioned the UFOC known as the Uniform Franchise Offering Circular. This is sometimes simply called the offering circular or prospectus. It was developed in 1975 by the Midwest Securities Commission Association and many states have also required the use of these more demanding regulations.

We will review the FTC rule in brief and then give an overview of the disclosures the UFOC will generally require. To minimize compliance regulations, the FTC allows the use of the UFOC format in lieu of its own disclosure rule, because the UFOC provides protection for franchisees that is equal or greater than that covered by the FTC rule. It is important to note that while a disclosure statement is required by law, there is no guarantee that it has been scrutinized by any regulatory agency for accuracy, and the FTC requires a statement in the disclosure document that informs one that the information given *has not* been verified.

THE FTC DISCLOSURE LIST

1. Information identifying the franchisor, any and all affiliates.

2. Information that identifies and describes the business experience of each of the franchisor's directors, offices and key executives.

3. The franchisor's business experience.

4. Litigation history of the franchisor, its directors and key executives.

5. Bankruptcy history of the franchisor and its directors and key executives.

6. Description of the franchise being offered for sale.

7. Initial funds to be paid by the franchisee.

8. Recurring funds required to be paid by the franchisee.

9. A list of persons with whom the franchisee is required or advised to do business with by the franchisor.

10. A statement describing any obligations to purchase.

11. Description of revenues to be received by the franchisor in consideration of purchases by the franchisee.

12. Description of financing arrangements.

13. Description of any restrictions of sale.

14. Required participation by the franchisee.

15. Termination, cancellation and renewal of the franchise.

16. Statistical information about the number of franchises and company-owned outlets.

17. Franchisor's site selection.

18. Training programs for the franchisee.

19. Public figure and celebrity involvement in the franchise.

20. Financial information about the franchisor.

As you can see, the FTC helps with some valuable information but we'll go into more detail regarding the UFOC format along with an overview. A substantial number of franchisors follow this form, and generally a UFOC will require the following disclosures.

UFOC DISCLOSURES AND EXPLANATION

In general, the UFOC requires information on:

1. *The Background of the Franchisor and Any Predecessors:* This is where the franchisor must disclose background, financial history, address, organization, and all predecessors of the franchising company. "Predecessor" is any previous business the franchisor operated in which there was a direct relationship to the franchise.

2. *Persons Affiliated with the Franchisor, to Include Franchise Broker:* This gives the identity and business background of all persons affiliated with the franchisor, such as owner, trustee, director, manager, principals, officers and/or other management companies. The biography of each person must be disclosed for the last five years.

3. *Litigation:* In this section, the franchisor is to disclose any litigation, criminal or civil, that involved any proceedings in violation of the franchise law or that would concern the potential franchisee. Details and status must be given.

4. *Bankruptcy:* If any of the franchisors, predecessors, officers, partners, etc. have filed for bankruptcy or reorganized due to insolvency during the past 15 years, it must be disclosed along with details of any action taken.

5. *Initial Fee or Other Payments:* This is where the amount of the franchise fee is given, along with the franchisor's refund policy and payment plan. You'll find that some franchisors offer no refund under any circumstances and others have a refund policy under certain conditions. A franchisor must also disclose the disposition of fees and all payments.

6. *Other Fees:* This is the section of the UFOC that discloses any other fees, such as royalty payments, advertising fund or pools, audits, equipment leases (if applicable), training and any other applicable fees. The franchisor must also give details on amounts and terms.

7. *Initial Investment:* Here you'll find a breakdown of the total initial investment that a franchisee can expect to have. It must also state exactly who receives payment, the terms and what is or is not refundable. These expenses may include but are not limited to fixtures, licensings, working capital (not always included), construction, architectural costs and supplies. If this estimated investment does not include "working capital" be sure to ask for an estimate and factor it in. Working capital is always needed to start up a business.

8. *Obligations of Franchisee to Purchase or Lease from Designated Sources:* This is where the franchisor must state if you will be required to purchase any equipment, products, services, goods, supplies, etc. from a designated source or from the franchisor. Also, the franchisor must disclose requirements to lease from a designated source, along with terms and any benefit the franchisor derives from the requirements for purchase or lease of such items.

9. *Obligations of Franchisee to Purchase or Lease in Accordance with Specifications or from Approved Suppliers:* Here the franchisor will disclose whether the franchisee will be required to buy or lease from pre-approved suppliers any supplies or products, etc. that are based on the franchisor's specifications. The actual specifications do not have to be given here; they are usually in the operating manual. Franchisors must disclose if they receive any compensation from approved suppliers as a result of the required transactions.

10. *Financing:* If any financing arrangements are offered by the franchisor or affiliates, the terms and conditions of such programs must be disclosed. Some franchisors will finance part or all of the investment, but most these days do not finance the franchisee.

11. *Obligations of the Franchisor:* In this section, the franchisor describes all services provided after the agreement is signed. This includes services provided as outlined in the franchise agreement and any that are offered at the discretion of the franchisor. The list will include supervision and assistance, services prior to opening the business, services while you're open, site selection assistance and other types of support and services.

12. *Exclusive Territorial Rights:* If you are to receive any exclusive or protected territorial rights, this is the section the franchisor will use to fully describe those rights and the territory itself. All conditions and rights of adjustment must be disclosed. If the franchisor has any exclusions, this will also be disclosed.

13. *Trademarks, Commercial Symbols, Logotypes, Service Marks and Trade Names:* The franchisor must disclose what legal steps have been taken to protect its trademarks, commercial symbols, logotypes, service marks and trade names. This is to include any federal government registrations and states and counties where registered. Description and artwork samples will be printed in this section along with restrictions or limitations for the franchisee in the use of such marks.

14. *Patents and Copyrights:* Any patents or copyrights involving the franchise are to be disclosed in this section.

15. *Obligation of the Franchise to Participate in the Operation of the Franchise Business:* Here the franchisor will state if there is to be active participation of the franchisee in the operation of the business. If this is the case, then terms must be outlined and all conditions explained. If you do not have to be active, then any requirements for management must be disclosed.

16. *Restrictions on Goods and Services Offered by the Franchise:* In this section of the disclosure document, the franchisor must disclose whether or not the franchisee will be limited as to the type and amounts of products and services that may be sold. Requirements on new products or service instructions should also be provided in this section.

17. *Renewal, Termination, Repurchase and Assignment:* You should review this section very closely. It defines the options and requirements for the franchise to be renewed, terminated, repurchased, modified or assigned. The conditions outlined here should be reviewed by an attorney familiar with franchise agreements. This section will cover other requirements and procedures involved in the modification of the franchise agreement.

18. *Arrangements with Public Figures:* This is where the franchisor will disclose any benefit or compensation that has been proved to a public figure in return for an endorsement by this public person. All details, arrangements, conditions and or limits must be disclosed about the use of the name or any endorsement by the public figure, including the rights of the franchisees as they relate to such activities.

19. *Representations Regarding Earnings Capability:* If the franchisor declines to provide any earnings statements of franchises, they must include a disclaimer to this effect. If the franchisor does make an earnings claim of sales and profits, then they must provide a factual description of this claim and the formula used to arrive at the claim.

20. *Information Regarding Franchises of the Franchisor:* In this section the franchisor provides a list of all the franchisees, along with their names, addresses, and telephone numbers. They must provide the number of franchises sold and number of those that are operating, the number of agreements/contracts signed for franchises that are not yet operating and how many company-owned franchise units there are. Another requirement is to disclose the number of franchises terminated, with explanations of the nonrenewals, for the past three years.

21. *Financial Statements:* A current financial statement which must be audited by a certified public accountant whose official stamp is visible on the document. Some states have additional requirements.

22. *Contracts:* Here you'll find a copy of the franchise agreement and any other related agreements that require a signature. These are enclosed as exhibits and are far more detailed than the disclosure statement.

REMEMBER: As we stated earlier, neither the FTC nor any other regulatory body will check the accuracy of the information you receive in the UFOC. When you evaluate a franchisor's disclosure document be sure to use your evaluation forms and your list of questions. We also highly recommend that you use the services of a qualified attorney.

Your Turn   *Complete the following activity:*

▶ Take some time out of your day and call a couple of franchise organizations that you think you may have an interest in and see how much information you can obtain or have sent to you before you have a face-to-face meeting.

EXAMPLE

The Case of "All that Glitters Is Not Gold"

Mr. and Mrs. Hays decided long ago that complete retirement wasn't for them. They both had thirty years service with a large international oil and gas firm, so they took early retirement with handsome pensions. Although they felt they could live their lives without financial worry, they knew they weren't the type to sit back and relax. So the Hayses purchased a franchise. The franchise agreement stated that the franchisor would select the site. The franchisor hired a realtor to pick the location and make the arrangements. (Mr. and Mrs. Hays did not know that most franchisors will only want to approve your site selection to determine if it meets their market area criteria.) The couple did not like the site selection and did not feel it would draw customers for their small costume jewelry retail franchise. They did their own detailed market analysis and proved to the franchisor that this was not an area to retail faux jewelry or anything else. The franchisor agreed. Another area was selected and proved to be a gold mine for the Hays family.

Much of the hassle could have been avoided if Mr. and Mrs. Hays:

1. Had done more research before signing the agreement.

2. Questioned the section on location and site selection.

3. Had a knowledgeable lawyer review the contract.

4. Asked for a market analysis for the proposed site in advance.

THE CONTENTS OF THE FRANCHISE AGREEMENT

Many franchise agreements will differ in their content but you'll find that they generally have the same elements. You'll also find that each part of the contract defines the relationship between franchisor and franchisee. It must confirm in greater detail the elements of the disclosure document. If there is any area of concern in the agreement it should be brought to the attention of your attorney.

You will find most contracts contain at least the following elements, if not more. Not necessarily in this order, you may find:

1. The recital.

2. Initial fees.

3. Ongoing fees.

4. Grants by the franchisor.

5. Terms of the agreement.

6. Services provided by the franchisor.

7. Agreements by the franchisee.

8. Rights to terminate the franchise agreement.

9. Obligations of the franchisee on termination.

10. Sale, transfer and assignment.

11. Insurance and indemnification.

12. Accounting and records.

13. Proprietary marks.

14. Appointment.

15. Term and renewal.

16. Advertising.

17. Taxes, permits and indebtedness.

18. Covenants.

19. Enforcement and construction.

20. Operating system.

21. Miscellaneous provisions.

22. Riders, amendments and addenda.

Once again, compare the disclosure document and the franchise agreement. Review and make sure you point out any differences before signing the contract.

We provided you with checklists and questions to ask the franchisor. We also gave you evaluation forms to use while evaluating your different franchise interests. Now we'll give you a checklist of a few of the things you should consider as you review your franchise agreement.

Make Sure You Understand

► Your obligations upon termination of the agreement.

► The franchisor's obligation upon termination of the agreement.

► The provisions of renewal.

► If the agreement permits the franchisor to audit your books and records.

► The types of reports you must submit.

► The conditions under which you can assign the franchise to someone else.

► If the franchisor will have right of first refusal to purchase if you want to sell.

► If you have the right to renew the franchise agreement when it expires.

► If you do renew, if you use the same agreement.

► All conditions for renewal.

► The terms and rights you have to terminate the contract.

► The operating standards.

► Your obligations to protect trade secrets.

► If you are restricted to certain business activities.

► The amount of the franchise fee.

► The amount or percentage that will be royalty fees.

► All rights granted to you and explanations.

► The advertising you'll receive and any co-op advertising fee you'll pay.

► If you receive training, and if it is only initial training or ongoing.

► Your territorial agreement.

► The entire agreement, including terms, covenants and provisions.

► Any limitations or restrictions to the contract.

► What type of ongoing assistance you'll receive from the franchisor.

► The provisions of site selection.

► The type and amount of insurance you'll need.

▶ Additional services that the franchisor is obligated to furnish.

▶ The time period allowed between the signing of the agreement and the opening.

▶ All costs to you for the construction and operation of the facility.

▶ Requirements for products and equipment.

▶ Any and all noncompetitive clauses.

▶ Procedures to follow if you should wish to relocate the franchise.

▶ The requirements and any conditions under which the franchisor will allow the transfer or sale of the franchise.

▶ The rights you have to pass interest on to heirs.

As you can see, the offering circular with franchise agreement can contain quite a lot of information. It is important to review every element in detail and to question any statement you don't understand. Many franchisors would like the franchisee to believe that their agreements have little or no room to negotiate. Some states require the franchisor to file any changes made to the agreement, but many allow room to negotiate. Understand the legal requirements of the state in which you'll locate the franchise and obtain the services of a good franchise attorney.

There are serious red flags to consider as you work with franchise representatives.

Beware:

- If any franchise representative refuses to answer questions or can't give you details.

- If you're promised anything that is not put in writing.

- If you don't receive a reference list when you ask for it.

- If you felt the franchise representative used pressure and unrealistic promises.

- If the franchise representative tries to get you to sign a contract before you can have your attorney review it.

- If you are asked to pay money before you receive a disclosure statement.

- If earnings claims are made without supporting documents.

- If you are made oral or written representations that are inconsistent with the disclosures made in the disclosure statement.

Needless to say, if any of the above should happen, mark this franchise off your list and move on.

ASK YOURSELF

► What are the main differences in the disclosure document and the franchise agreement (contract)?

► Do you know what to look for in an offering circular?

► Why should you have a franchise lawyer review all documents before you sign anything?

CHAPTER FIVE

WHAT YOU CAN EXPECT TO SEE: Documents from the Business

IN THE REAL WORLD

"Chance favors the prepared mind."
—Louis Pasteur

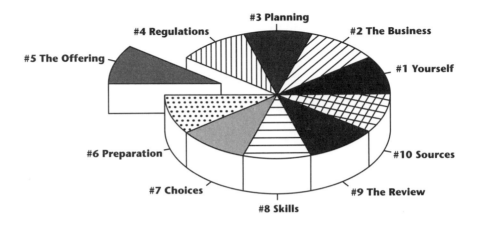

On the following pages of this book you'll find a sample of a real offering circular. As you review the documents, look back to the previous chapter for any references and an explanation of each of the sections. Some exclusions have been made and are noted in the circular. The offering circular provided comes from Wicks 'N' Sticks with permission to reprint in this book.

Wicks 'N' Sticks was chosen for the sample offering circular because of its clear and concise documents. It is an example of an established franchisor with over 25 years of experience and it is an excellent example of a franchisor who does a great job providing the disclosure regulations that they are required to give to prospective franchisees.

We believe that seeing an actual offering circular will help you become better prepared for what lies ahead as you begin your quest to own your first franchise.

WICKS N STICKS

UNIFORM FRANCHISE OFFERING CIRCULAR

WICKS 'N' STICKS, INC.
INFORMATION FOR PROSPECTIVE FRANCHISEES
REQUIRED BY THE FEDERAL TRADE COMMISSION

* * * * *

To protect you, we've required your franchisor to give you this information. *We haven't checked it and don't know if it's correct.* It should help you make up your mind. Study it carefully. While it includes some information about your contract, don't rely on it alone to understand your contract. Read all of your contract carefully. Buying a franchise is a complicated investment. Take your time to decide. If possible, show your contract and this information to an advisor, like a lawyer or an accountant. If you find anything you think may be wrong or anything important that's been left out, you should let us know about it. It may be against the law.

There may also be laws on franchising in your state. Ask your state agencies about them.

Federal Trade Commission
Washington, D.C. 20580

CALIFORNIA, HAWAII, ILLINOIS, INDIANA, MARYLAND, MICHIGAN, MINNESOTA, NEW YORK, NORTH DAKOTA, RHODE ISLAND, SOUTH DAKOTA, VIRGINIA, WASHINGTON, AND WISCONSIN REQUIRE FRANCHISORS TO MAKE ADDITIONAL DISCLOSURES RELATED TO THE INFORMATION CONTAINED IN THIS OFFERING CIRCULAR. IF APPLICABLE, THESE ADDITIONAL DISCLOSURES WILL BE FURNISHED TO YOU IN AN ADDENDUM TO THIS OFFERING CIRCULAR.

IN ACCORDANCE WITH THE REQUIREMENTS OF THE FEDERAL TRADE COMMISSION, THIS OFFERING CIRCULAR WAS ISSUED ON MAY 7, 1993. IF THIS OFFERING CIRCULAR IS REGISTERED IN A STATE LISTED ABOVE, THE EFFECTIVE DATE OF THIS OFFERING WILL BE DISCLOSED IN THE ADDENDUM FOR THAT STATE.

UNIFORM FRANCHISE OFFERING CIRCULAR

OF

Wicks 'N' Sticks Franchise

TABLE OF CONTENTS

Wicks 'N' Sticks Uniform Franchise Offering Circular
Effective May 7, 1993.

Exhibits

APPLICABLE STATE LAW MAY REQUIRE ADDITIONAL DISCLOSURES RELATED TO THE INFORMATION IN THIS OFFERING CIRCULAR. THESE ADDITIONAL DISCLOSURES, IF ANY, APPEAR IN AN ADDENDUM.

Wicks 'N' Sticks Uniform Franchise Offering Circular
Effective May 7, 1993.

ITEM I

THE COMPANY AND ANY PREDECESSORS

The Company: Wicks 'N' Sticks, Inc. (hereinafter referred to as "Company") is a Delaware corporation, incorporated September 29, 1981, doing business as Wicks 'N' Sticks, and maintaining its principal office at 16825 Northchase Drive, Suite 900, Houston, Texas 77060 (P.O. Box 4586, Houston, Texas 77210-4586).

The Company's Business: The Company is a retail specialty company which grants franchises for the operation of retail stores known as Wicks 'N' Sticks. As of April 30, 1993, there were 189 franchised Wicks 'N' Sticks locations and four (4) Company-owned Wicks 'N' Sticks locations in operation in 39 states. The franchise offered pursuant to this offering circular licenses a franchisee (hereinafter referred to as "Franchisee") to operate a Wicks 'N' Sticks store. The Company offers prospective franchisees the opportunity to purchase a Wicks 'N' Sticks store within a designated market area within a specified time period by entering into a Franchise Option Agreement (Exhibit "F").

The Wicks 'N' Sticks Franchise: A Wicks 'N' Sticks store is a retail establishment devoted primarily to the sale of candles, candle accessories, room fragrances, room fragrance accessories, wedding and special occasion keepsakes, and other related decorative accessories and services. Each store is operated pursuant to the Company's unique system (hereinafter referred to as "System"), which includes, but is not limited to, special merchandising, specially designed facilities, interior and exterior layout and trade dress, standards and specifications for fixtures and equipment, methods for keeping books and records, inventory control systems, training supervision, and field operations support, all of which may be changed, improved, and updated by the Company. The Company also offers Franchisees the opportunity to operate kiosks within the mall in which the franchised Wicks 'N' Sticks store is located during the Christmas holiday season.

The Franchisee will compete with other stores offering products and services similar to those offered by the Wicks 'N' Sticks stores, including department stores and specialty stores.

Prior Business Experience: The Company has franchised and/or operated Wicks 'N' Sticks retail stores selling candles, decorative accessories, and related products since January 1, 1993.

Wicks 'N' Sticks Uniform Franchise Offering Circular
Effective May 7, 1993.

The Company's Predecessor: The Company's predecessor, WNS, Inc. was founded in 1968 and was incorporated under the laws of the State of Texas in 1969. WNS, Inc. began franchising and operating Wicks 'N' Sticks retail stores selling candles, decorative accessories, and related products in October, 1968. WNS, Inc. began operating retail stores selling frames, prints, and related products in August, 1979, and franchising retail stores under the name "Deck the Walls" in 1982. In April, 1986, WNS, Inc. purchased substantially all of the assets of Wallpapers To Go, Inc., a California corporation, and began franchising and/or operating Wallpapers To Go retail stores selling wallcoverings and related products. In January, 1990, WNS, Inc. sold substantially all of the assets of the Deck The Walls division to a group led by John W. Jones, former president of WNS, Inc. On January 31, 1992, WNS, Inc. and its wholly-owned subsidiaries, Wicks 'N' Sticks, Inc. and Wallpapers To Go, Inc., filed a voluntary petition for financial reorganization under Chapter 11 of the United States Code. As a result of WNS, Inc.'s bankruptcy proceeding, the Wicks 'N' Sticks franchise agreements were assigned to the Company by WNS, Inc. effective January 1, 1993. The Wallpapers To Go franchise agreements were assigned to Wallpapers To Go, Inc. by WNS, Inc. effective January 1, 1993. WNS, Inc.'s principal business address is 16825 Northchase Drive, Suite 900, Houston, Texas 77060.

Reference herein to the masculine, feminine, or neuter gender is for convenience only and reference to one gender includes all others.

ITEM II

IDENTITY AND BUSINESS EXPERIENCE OF PERSONS
AFFILIATED WITH THE COMPANY

The following is a list of directors, principal officers, and other employees who have management responsibilities in connection with the operation of the Company's business relating to the franchises described in this offering circular. The principal occupation and business experience of each person during the past five years is described below. The officers listed below have served in their current position with the Company since December 17, 1992. Except as described below, the managers listed have served in their current position with the Company since January 1, 1993.

1) William D. Sivitz
   Chief Executive Officer,
   Director

Mr. Sivitz joined the Company, Wallpapers To Go, Inc., and WNS, Inc. as Chief Executive Officer on December 17, 1992. He has been a partner of Princeton Investment Partners since January, 1988. He became a Director of Rexon Technology Corporation in April, 1989, and a Director and Chairman of the Board of Seasons, Inc. in June, 1990.

Wicks 'N' Sticks Uniform Franchise Offering Circular
Effective May 7, 1993.

2) D. Ross Arthurs
   Chief Financial Officer,
   Director
	Mr. Arthurs joined the Company, Wallpapers To Go, Inc., and WNS, Inc. as Chief Financial Officer on December 17, 1992. He has been a partner of Princeton Investment Partners since January, 1992. He was Vice President and a partner of TMB Industries from March, 1989, through December, 1991. He was president of the Imperial Division of The Pullman Company from September, 1987, through March, 1989.

3) Stanley D. Slap Director, Consultant	Mr. Slap has served as a Director of the Company and of Wallpapers To Go, Inc. since December 17, 1992. He has also served as a Director of WNS, Inc. since May 1, 1992. He serves as a Consultant for the Company, Wallpapers To Go, Inc., and WNS, Inc. He served as President of WNS, Inc. from May 1, 1992, through May 6, 1993, and served as President of the Company and of Wallpapers To Go, Inc. from December 17, 1992, through May 6, 1993. He is the founder of Retail Revealed, a consulting firm, and has served as its President since its inception in September, 1985.
4) Dennis B. Dickison Vice President	Mr. Dickison joined WNS, Inc. as Vice President, Wicks 'N' Sticks Operations in January, 1982. In January, 1990, he was named Vice President, Wicks 'N' Sticks division. He was named Vice President of the Company on December 17, 1992.

5) T. Deanne Carlisle
   Vice President-Finance
   Secretary-Treasurer
	Ms. Carlisle joined WNS, Inc. in October, 1986, and was named Vice President-Controller/Secretary-Treasurer in January, 1990. She was named Vice President-Finance/Secretary-Treasurer of the Company, of Wallpapers To Go, Inc., and of WNS, Inc. on December 17, 1992.

6) Deborah F. Steinberg
   Vice President/Franchise
   Development
	Ms. Steinberg was employed by WNS, Inc. as a Regional Manager from January, 1983, to June, 1988. She was employed by Supercuts, Incorporated as Vice President from June, 1988, to January, 1990.

Wicks 'N' Sticks Uniform Franchise Offering Circular
Effective May 7, 1993.

She rejoined WNS, Inc. as Vice President, Wallpapers To Go in January, 1990. She was named Vice President-Franchise Development of the Company and of Wallpapers To Go, Inc. on December 17, 1992.

7) Roger Fussner
   Regional Manager

Mr. Fussner has been a Wicks 'N' Sticks franchisee since July, 1976. In January, 1989, he joined WNS, Inc. as a Regional Manager.

8) Daryl W. Newton
   Regional Manager

Mr. Newton joined WNS, Inc. as the Manager of Construction Design in November, 1987. He has been a Regional Manager since January, 1990.

9) Greg E. Sever
   Regional Manager

Mr. Sever joined WNS, Inc. as a Regional Manager in June, 1989. From August, 1986, to May, 1989, he was employed by Bakers Stationers, Inc., as Vice President, Store Operations.

10) Diane L. Stites
    Regional Manager

Ms. Stites joined WNS, Inc. as a Regional Coordinator in August, 1990. From January, 1993, to February, 1993, she served as a Regional Coordinator for the Company and has been a Regional Manager since February, 1993. Prior to joining WNS, Inc., she was the Owner/Operator of Retail Concepts Group from June, 1989, through June, 1990. She was employed by Paul Harris Store, Inc. as Senior District Manager from August, 1984, through June, 1989.

11) Lisa A. Wolpers
    Regional Manager

Ms. Wolpers joined WNS, Inc. as a Deck The Walls Corporate Store Manager in September, 1985. She was the Director of Corporate Stores for Deck The Walls and Wicks 'N' Sticks from May, 1987, through July, 1989. Between July, 1989, and February, 1990, she worked as an Independent Contractor managing four Deck The Walls stores. In February, 1990, she became a Regional Coordinator and Training Director for the Wicks 'N' Sticks division. From January, 1993, to February, 1993,

Wicks 'N' Sticks Uniform Franchise Offering Circular
Effective May 7, 1993.

she served as a Regional Coordinator for the Company and has been a Regional Manager since February, 1993.

12) Peggy Hager
    Communications
    Manager

Ms. Hager joined WNS, Inc. in June, 1979, and works as communications liaison with franchisees.

13) Judy L. Wahlberg
    New Store Operations
    Manager

Ms. Wahlberg joined WNS, Inc. in April, 1979. She became New Store Operations Manager in September, 1987, and handles store design and training.

14) Terri K. Martinez
    Merchandise Manager

Ms. Martinez began working in Wicks 'N' Sticks stores on a part time basis in 1973. She managed Wicks 'N' Sticks stores from May, 1979, until February, 1986, when she became a Regional Operations Coordinator for WNS, Inc. She has been a Merchandise Manager since January, 1989.

15) Colleen B. Booth
    Merchandise Manager

Ms. Booth joined WNS, Inc. as a Special Projects Manager in June, 1990. She has been a Merchandise Manager since December, 1991. Prior to joining WNS, Inc., she was a student at Texas A&M University.

ITEM III

LITIGATION

Neither the Company nor any person identified in Item II above:

A.   Has any administrative, criminal, material civil action, or material arbitration proceeding (or a significant number of civil actions or arbitration proceedings, irrespective of materiality) pending against them alleging a violation of any franchise law, fraud, embezzlement, fraudulent conversion, restraint of trade, unfair or deceptive practices, misappropriation of property, or comparable allegations.

B.   Has, during the ten (10) year period immediately preceding the date of the offering circular, been convicted of a felony or pleaded *nolo contendere* to a felony

Wicks 'N' Sticks Uniform Franchise Offering Circular
Effective May 7, 1993.

charge or been held liable in a civil action by final judgment or been held liable in any arbitration proceeding or been the subject of a material complaint or other legal proceedings involving violation of any franchise law, fraud, embezzlement, fraudulent conversion, restraint of trade, unfair or deceptive practices, misappropriation of property, or comparable allegations.

C. Is subject to any currently effective injunctive or restrictive order or decree relating to the franchise or under any federal, state, or Canadian franchise, securities, antitrust, trade regulation, or trade practice law as a result of a concluded or pending action or proceeding brought by a public agency.

The above descriptions do not include proceedings against the Company's predecessor, WNS, Inc. WNS, Inc. has, within the ten (10) year period immediately preceding the date of this offering circular, been a party to lawsuits involving the above-described allegations. To the extent the claims in such lawsuits were not satisfied prior to the filing by WNS, Inc. of a petition in bankruptcy (see Item IV., below) such claims were or will be resolved in a bankruptcy proceeding. These claims were or will be discharged or satisfied by payment of a pro rata share of preferred stock which has been set aside for successful claimants. As a result of the bankruptcy proceeding, neither WNS, Inc., nor the Company, will be required to make a monetary payment to any such claimant.

ITEM IV

BANKRUPTCY

On January 31, 1992, the Company and its predecessor, WNS, Inc. filed voluntary petitions for financial reorganization under Chapter 11 of the United States Code in the United States Bankruptcy Court for the Southern District of Texas, Houston Division ("Bankruptcy Court"). The reorganizations were jointly administered as Case No. 92-40938-H1-11. The Bankruptcy Court confirmed the Company's Third Amended Joint Plan of Reorganization (the "Plan") on November 5, 1992, and the Company emerged from Chapter 11 reorganization on December 16, 1992. In accordance with certain provisions in the Plan, the assets and liabilities of the Wicks 'N' Sticks operating division were transferred from WNS, Inc. to the Company.

Except as set forth above, during the fifteen (15) year period immediately preceding the date of this offering circular, neither the Company nor any predecessor, current officer, or general partner of the Company has been adjudged bankrupt or reorganized due to insolvency or been a principal officer of a company or a general partner of a partnership at or within one (1) year of the time that such company or partnership was adjudged bankrupt or reorganized due to insolvency or is otherwise subject to any such pending bankruptcy or reorganization proceeding.

Wicks 'N' Sticks Uniform Franchise Offering Circular
Effective May 7, 1993.

ITEM V

THE FRANCHISEE'S INITIAL FRANCHISE FEE OR OTHER INITIAL PAYMENT

Initial Franchise Fee: In connection with the purchase of a new store location, the Franchisee will pay the Company an initial franchise fee of $25,000 prior to the Franchisee's execution of the Franchise Agreement. If the Franchisee currently owns one or more Wicks 'N' Sticks franchised businesses, the initial franchise fee will be $15,000. There is no provision in the Franchise Agreement which entitles a Franchisee to a refund of any portion of the initial franchise fee.

Franchise Option Fee: In the event the prospective franchisee enters into a Franchise Option Agreement (Exhibit "F"), he will pay the Company a franchise option fee in the amount of $5,000. Such fee is due at the time the prospective franchisee executes the Franchise Option Agreement and is credited toward the franchise fee. This fee is uniform in all cases and may be refundable under certain circumstances.

Use of Proceeds: The franchise fees are used to pay or defray some of the following expenses:

1.   Obtaining and screening franchisees;

2.   Screening, selecting and negotiating sites;

3.   Lease review;

4.   Assistance in site development;

5.   Assistance and supervision provided by the Company for the opening of the franchised store;

6.   The training program for two (2) persons who will own and/or manage the franchised business;

7.   Any expenses incurred in connection with the protection of proprietary marks designated for use in connection with the franchise offered;

8.   Employee salaries and expenses with respect to the preparation of this franchise offering circular and in connection with the marketing, real estate, and selling activities relating to the franchises being offered;

9.   Development expenses relating to the development and improvement of the System, including standards, procedures, techniques, and other elements of such System;

Wicks 'N' Sticks Uniform Franchise Offering Circular
Effective May 7, 1993.

10.   On-going development of plans and specifications for store layout and decor; and

11.   Legal fees, accounting fees, and fees incurred to comply with federal, state, and other laws with respect to the preparation and/or filing of this franchise offering circular.

ITEM VI

OTHER FEES AND EXPENSES

Continuing Royalty Fee: The continuing royalty fee is applied toward the Company's expenses in providing Franchisees with field support and operations management. The Franchisee will pay the Company a continuing royalty fee of six percent (6%) of the Franchisee's gross sales of all goods and services. Gross sales of all goods and services include the dollar aggregate of the sales price on all goods, wares, merchandise, and services sold by the Franchisee. The continuing royalty fee is based on the previous month's gross sales and is to be received on or before the tenth (10th) day of each month. The continuing royalty fee is nonrefundable and is not collected on behalf of nor paid to any third party.

Minimum Rent and Other Lease Charges: The Franchisee will pay minimum rent and other lease charges for the franchised location as required by the lease and/or sublease agreement. The minimum rent and other lease charges will vary depending on factors which include, but are not limited to, the location and size of the store. The Company is unable to estimate the exact minimum rent and other lease charges for a particular location. The minimum rent and other lease charges are usually payable to the lessor under the lease (hereinafter referred to as "Lessor") and are nonrefundable.

Training Costs: The cost of the instruction and required materials incurred in connection with the initial training program is borne by the Company. All other expenses including, but not limited to, those for accommodations, travel, and wages of the persons to be trained are borne by the Franchisee. Additional training programs may be provided by the Company from time to time for which the Company will bear only the costs of instruction and required materials. The Franchisee, at his own expense, conducts training classes for his employees regarding sales and maintenance techniques as may be prescribed by the Company in the Confidential Training/Operations Manual or otherwise in writing.

Wicks 'N' Sticks Uniform Franchise Offering Circular
Effective May 7, 1993.

Insurance: The Franchisee is required to purchase the following types of insurance at his expense, through licensed insurance companies acceptable to the Company, and will maintain such insurance in effect at all times during the term of the Franchise Agreement:

1.   Broad form comprehensive general liability coverage and broad form contractual liability coverage;

2.   Worker's Compensation and Employer's Liability Insurance;

3.   Unemployment Insurance;

4.   Fire and Extended Coverage Insurance;

5.   Business Interruption Insurance; and

6.   State Disability Insurance.

The minimum limits of insurance coverage required to be procured by the Franchisee may be modified from time to time by the Company upon written notice to the Franchisee.

If the Franchisee does not purchase insurance conforming to the standards and limits prescribed by the Company, the Company may (but is not required to) obtain such insurance on behalf of the Franchisee. The Franchisee will be required to reimburse the Company for all expenses incurred in obtaining such insurance upon receipt of a billing for same. Except for insurance obtained for the Franchisee by the Company, no payment for insurance is collected or imposed by the Company in whole or in part on behalf of, nor paid to any third party, except as may be required pursuant to the terms of the lease for the franchised location. Insurance costs may not be uniform as to all persons currently acquiring a franchise since premiums may differ depending on factors which include, but are not limited to, the insurer, the location, the insurance requirements of applicable law, and lease requirements.

Audit Costs: The Company has the right to audit and make copies of the Franchisee's books, records, accounts, and other documents. If such audit reveals that the gross sales are understated by one percent (1%) or more (provided such understatement exceeds $1,000), the Franchisee will pay and/or reimburse the Company for any and all expenses associated with the audit, including, but not limited to, accounting and legal fees, and expenses related to copying the Franchisee's books, records, accounts, and other documents.

Wicks 'N' Sticks Uniform Franchise Offering Circular
Effective May 7, 1993.

Franchise Transfer Fee: In the event the Franchisee sells or transfers all or any part of his interest in the franchise to any purchaser or transferee, he is required to pay a transfer fee in the amount of Three Thousand Dollars ($3,000). Such fee is to be received by the Company prior to the effective date of the sale or transfer. This fee is uniform in all cases, is nonrefundable, and is not collected in whole or in part on behalf of nor paid to any third party. The Company may, upon the Franchisee's request, assist the Franchisee in locating a suitable purchaser for the Franchisee's Wicks 'N' Sticks store.

Relocation Expenses: In the event the Franchisee has not had the opportunity to operate the store at the franchised location for the initial term of the Franchise Agreement due to expiration or termination of the lease, or if the premises is damaged, condemned, or otherwise rendered unusable, and provided he has fully complied with the terms of the Franchise Agreement, the Franchisee may relocate the franchise to another site if: (1) the site has been approved by the Company in writing (which approval will not be unreasonably withheld); (2) such store is opened within one (1) year from the date the store at the franchised location is closed; and (3) the store appearance of the new location is in accordance with the Company's then-current requirements. If the Franchisee relocates his store to a new site, he may be required to pay to the Company an administrative fee not to exceed twenty percent (20%) of the then-current initial franchise fee. Such administrative fee must be received prior to the effective date of the relocation. Any costs associated with such relocation will be at the Franchisee's expense.

Taxes: Any sales, use, or other tax imposed on amounts paid to the Company pursuant to the terms of the Franchise Agreement will be paid by the Franchisee within ten (10) days after notice that such amounts are due and owing.

Security Deposit: Upon execution of the Sublease Agreement, if applicable, the Franchisee may be required to deposit with the Company a security deposit equal to one (1) monthly installment of minimum rent and other lease charges. This fee may be refundable pursuant to the terms of the Sublease Agreement (Exhibit "E") and is not collected in whole or in part on behalf of nor paid to any third party, except to the extent that the Company may pay the same to the Lessor.

Manual Replacement Fee: In the event the Franchisee's copy of the Confidential Training/Operations Manual is damaged, lost, or becomes out of date or unusable, the Franchisee will pay the Company a replacement fee of $50. This fee is nonrefundable and is not collected in whole or in part on behalf of nor paid to any third party.

Wicks 'N' Sticks Franchise Offering Circular
Effective May 7, 1993.

Interest: Interest may be charged (at the minimum rate allowed by law) on any past due amount owed to the Company. Interest charges are nonrefundable and are not collected in whole or in part on behalf of nor paid to any third party.

ITEM VII

THE FRANCHISEE'S ESTIMATED INITIAL INVESTMENT
AND OTHER FINANCIAL OBLIGATIONS

Estimated initial investment for a new store location in an existing mall:

CATEGORY OF INVESTMENT	AMOUNT	WHEN DUE	TO WHOM PAYMENT IS TO BE MADE
Initial Franchise Fee	$ 15,000 – $ 25,000 (Note 1)	Prior to execution of the Franchise Agreement	Company
Travel and Living Expenses while Training	$ 500 – $ 3,000	As incurred	Airlines, Hotels, Restaurants
Inventory and Supplies (including inbound freight charges)	$ 42,500 – $ 55,000 (Note 2)	According to payment terms	Suppliers (including carriers of Suppliers)
Fixtures and Equipment	$ 15,000 – $ 25,000	According to payment terms	Contractors and/or Suppliers
Leasehold Improvements	$ 25,000 – $ 50,000 (Note 3)	According to payment terms	Suppliers and/or Contractors
Architect's Fee	$ 2,500 – $ 5,000	According to payment terms	Architect
Working capital	$ 10,000 – $ 20,000 (Note 4)	As needed	Employees, Creditors and Suppliers
TOTAL (excluding Minimum Rent and Other Lease Charges)	$110,500 – $183,000		

Wicks 'N' Sticks Franchise Offering Circular
Effective May 7, 1993.

Note 1: The initial franchise fee for a Franchisee's purchase of his first Wicks 'N' Sticks franchise is $25,000. The initial franchise fee for additional Wicks 'N' Sticks franchises is $15,000 each.

Note 2: In the event the store opens during the months of October, November, or December, the cost of inventory, supplies, and freight will increase substantially as a result of the fact that a Wicks 'N' Sticks store typically experiences approximately fifty percent (50%) of its annual business during the months of October, November, and December.

Note 3: The costs for leasehold improvements may be higher ($50,000 - $70,000) for a store being built in a newly constructed mall or space.

Note 4: The estimates for working capital represent the amounts the Company estimates the Franchisee should have available during the start-up and development stage of the Wicks 'N' Sticks franchised business to cover expenses and operating costs in excess of revenues. Such estimates do not include provisions for the Franchisee's salary. The Franchisee must have either made other provisions for living expenses or have additional sums available, whether in cash, through a bank line of credit, or from an additional income source other than the Wicks 'N' Sticks store, to cover the Franchisee's living expenses during the start-up and development stage of the Wicks 'N' Sticks store. The amount of such additional reserves will vary greatly depending upon a number of factors, including but not limited to, the Franchisee's standard of living, the time of year the store opens, the amount of payroll expenses, minimum rent and other lease charges, and the amount of debt service, as well as the rate of growth and success of the Wicks 'N' Sticks store, which in turn will depend upon numerous factors including economic conditions of the area in which the Wicks 'N' Sticks store is located, the Wicks 'N' Sticks store's gross revenues, the Franchisee's ability to operate the Wicks 'N' Sticks store efficiently and in accordance with the Confidential Training/Operations Manual. The Company cannot meaningfully estimate when revenues will equal or exceed the cost of operation for the Wicks 'N' Sticks store. Actual working capital needs should be determined by a projected capital requirement and initial cash flow statement prepared by the Franchisee for his specific location.

The estimated initial investment to be made by the Franchisee in connection with the purchase of his store location in an existing mall may range from approximately $110,500 to $183,000 depending upon factors which include, but are not limited to, the size of the store, the amount of inventory and supplies, the cost of leasehold improvements, fixtures and equipment, the amount of freight charges, and other costs that may vary from one location to another. In certain circumstances, the actual costs may be higher due to factors which include, but are not limited to, additional requirements imposed by the Lessor, the time of year the store opens, and the amount of payroll expenses. The initial franchise fee is described in *Item V* and any financing arrangements with the Company are described in *Item X*.

THERE ARE NO OTHER DIRECT OR INDIRECT PAYMENTS TO THE COMPANY IN CONJUNCTION WITH THE PURCHASE OF THE FRANCHISE.

Wicks 'N' Sticks Franchise Offering Circular
Effective May 7, 1993.

ITEM VIII

OBLIGATIONS OF THE FRANCHISEE TO PURCHASE OR LEASE FROM DESIGNATED SOURCES

Except as described in *Item IX,* if the Franchisee purchases a new franchise, he may purchase or lease any goods, services, supplies, fixtures and equipment from any source, provided the Franchisee conforms to the Company's specifications and quality standards. The Company does not derive revenue from the purchases referred to above.

If the Franchisee purchases an existing Company-owned store, the leasehold improvements, fixtures and equipment, inventory, supplies, and signs at the location will be purchased from the Company. Such purchases from the Company represent virtually 100% of the Franchisee's total initial investment in connection with the purchase of such assets. The Franchisee may also be required to sublease the premises from the Company. The Company will extend the same terms as those contained in the lease for said premises. The Company may derive revenue from the sale of the assets referred to above.

The Company has the right to review the lease for the franchised business prior to execution by the Franchisee. Such lease shall include language allowing the Company the right to assume the lease in the event of the Franchisee's default or upon termination of the Franchise Agreement and allowing a successor franchisee the right to assume the lease in the event the Franchisee sells the franchise.

ITEM IX

OBLIGATIONS OF THE FRANCHISEE TO PURCHASE OR LEASE IN ACCORDANCE WITH SPECIFICATIONS OR FROM APPROVED SUPPLIERS

Real Property: When the location for a franchised store has been approved by the Company, the Franchisee will execute a lease for the franchised location. The Franchisee will provide the Company with a copy of the fully executed lease within ninety (90) days of the date of the Franchise Agreement, and open the store within one (1) year of the date of the Franchise Agreement. If the Franchisee does not provide the Company with a copy of the fully executed lease within ninety (90) days of the date of the Franchise Agreement and/or does not open his store within one (1) year of the date of the Franchise Agreement, the Franchisee will be deemed to be in default

Wicks 'N' Sticks Franchise Offering Circular
Effective May 7, 1993.

of the Franchise Agreement and the Company may terminate the Franchise Agreement upon thirty (30) days written notice unless the default is cured within said thirty (30) day period.

When the Franchisee executes the lease or other agreement for the franchised location:

1.   The Franchisee will not create or purport to create any obligations on behalf of the Company, nor grant or purport to grant to the Lessor thereunder any rights against the Company, nor agree to any other term, condition, or covenant which is inconsistent with any provision of the Franchise Agreement;

2.   The Franchisee will duly and timely perform all of the terms, conditions, covenants, and obligations imposed upon him under the lease;

3.   Except as otherwise provided in the Franchise Agreement, the Franchisee may not assign the lease or sublease the franchised location or any portion thereof without the express prior written approval of the Company.

Any such lease or other agreement is required to be approved by the Company and will provide that:

1.   In the event of expiration or termination of the Franchise Agreement for any reason whatsoever, the Company has the option for thirty (30) days thereafter (a) to assume the obligations of and replace the Franchisee as the lessee under said lease, (b) to, within a reasonable period of time, cure any defaults thereunder, and (c) at any time thereafter to assign the lease or sublet the location to another Franchisee;

2.   The Lessor will furnish to the Company written notice specifying any default and the method of curing any such default under such lease and shall allow the Company thirty (30) days after receipt thereof to cure such default (except that if such default is in the nature of non-payment of rent and other lease charges, the Company shall have fifteen (15) days from receipt of such notice to cure such default) and allow the Company to exercise its option to succeed to the Franchisee's interest in such lease;

3.   The Lessor will accept the Company as a substitute lessee under the terms and provisions of the lease upon notice from the Company that it is exercising its option to succeed to the interest of the Franchisee in such lease;

4.   The Lessor acknowledges that the Franchisee is responsible for all debts, payments, and performance due under said lease prior to the time that the Company is given actual possession of the premises pursuant to its rights in such lease;

Wicks 'N' Sticks Franchise Offering Circular
Effective May 7, 1993.

5.   All of the foregoing constitute rights but not obligations on the part of the Company to assume the rights and responsibilities of the Franchisee under any lease or other agreement;

6.   The Franchisee is permitted to display the Company's standard signage and displays relating to the conduct of the franchised business; and

7.   It may not be modified or amended without the Company's prior written approval, which approval will not be unreasonably withheld. The Company will be promptly provided with copies of all such proposed modifications or amendments and, when executed, true and correct copies of such executed modifications and amendments.

Inventory, Fixtures, Equipment, and Supplies: To ensure uniformity and quality, the Franchisee is required to purchase or lease all products, supplies, equipment, and materials required for the operation of the franchised business from suppliers who: (1) demonstrate, to the Company's satisfaction, the ability to meet all the Company's standards and specifications for such items; (2) utilize a satisfactory quality control system; (3) possess adequate capacity and facilities to supply the Franchisee's needs in the quantities, at the times, and with the reliability requisite to an efficient operation; (4) maintain adequate liability insurance in amounts determined by the Company; and (5) have been approved in writing by the Company and continue to be in good and approved standing.

The Franchisee is required to submit to the Company (prior to purchasing any merchandise) a written request for approval of any supplier not previously approved by the Company. As a condition for such approval, the Franchisee or supplier will furnish samples of the merchandise to the Company for inspection and testing.

The Company may require the Franchisee or the supplier, if approved, to pay any expenses incurred by the Company in connection with the approval process.

The Company does not directly manufacture or supply any inventory. However, there are some trademarked products licensed by or manufactured for the Company which are essential to the System and the Franchisee is required to purchase such products as specified by the Company. The Company does not derive any revenue from the sale of such merchandise to the Franchisee.

Wicks 'N' Sticks Franchise Offering Circular
Effective May 7, 1993.

ITEM X

ITEM X

FINANCING ARRANGEMENTS

At the present time, the Company does not offer direct financing for the Franchisee's purchases of leasehold improvements, equipment, fixtures, inventory, supplies, or for any working capital requirements in connection with the Franchisee's purchase of a new store. The Franchisee is encouraged to seek any required financing from lending institutions or agencies of his own choosing. If requested by the Franchisee, the Company will consult with him regarding financial assistance. The Company may offer financing in connection with the Franchisee's purchase of Company-owned stores. In addition, financing may be available to veterans (as described in *Item XI.*).

Upon the Franchisee's request, the Company will assist the Franchisee in obtaining financing by providing the Franchisee with information concerning financing sources, preparation of a loan proposal and preparation of a business plan. The Company does not, however, have any arrangement with a lender for the provision of financing for a Franchisee. In no event will the Company guaranty all or part of the Franchisee's obligations. The Company does not place financing with anyone, and therefore, does not receive any payment for the placement of financing.

The Company participates in the Veterans Transition Franchise Initiative (VETFRAN), which is a cosponsored program between the International Franchise Association and the VETFRAN Committee Chairman. The program is designed to assist veterans in purchasing a franchised business with reduced capital requirements. The Company anticipates that in connection with such assistance, the Company and the Franchisee will execute an unsecured note in the amount of one-half of the then-current franchise fee to be financed over a period of five (5) years at an interest rate of two percent (2%) above the prime rate recorded by a designated financial institution. The Company began offering this program in March, 1993. As of the date of this offering circular, no franchisee has participated in this program. The Company does not maintain a form agreement for such financing arrangement.

ITEM XI

OBLIGATIONS OF THE COMPANY, OTHER SUPERVISION, ASSISTANCE, OR SERVICES

Pre-Opening Obligations: The obligations to be performed by the Company prior to the opening of the franchised business are:

Wicks 'N' Sticks Franchise Offering Circular
Effective May 7, 1993.

1.   <u>Training Program:</u> The Company provides at least a five (5) day initial training program for two (2) persons designated by the Franchisee who are the owners and/or principal operators of the franchised business, pursuant to Article IV.A., page D-3 of the Franchise Agreement (Exhibit "D"). Such training program is held at the Company's headquarters in Houston, Texas, or at the Franchisee's store, with the location to be designated by the Company. Additionally, the Company may provide the Franchisee with an additional five (5) to ten (10) days' training in a designated store. As of the date of this offering circular, Lisa Wolpers, who has been working with the Company's Franchisees and/or Company personnel since September, 1985, is responsible for coordinating the training program for the Franchisees. The initial training program consists of seminar sessions led by the Company's personnel. Seminars may cover such topics as the duties and responsibilities of the Franchisee, the Company, and the Company's field personnel as they relate to franchise operations; merchandising matters such as the selection of products to be sold in the Franchisee's store; franchise meetings, buying shows, and the benefits derived therefrom; explanation of merchandising policies and procedures including merchandise displays, inventory procedures, ordering procedures, routing of merchandise, and vendor relations; inventory control, display and stock rotation; an explanation of sales reports, and purchase orders; personnel matters, including payroll-related forms and reports; explanation of proper in-store opening and closing procedures, operation of cash register, balancing of Daily Sales Reports, in-store records; and business ethics. The training program may change from time to time and no representation is made that all such matters will be presented at training sessions. The initial training session is usually scheduled prior to the date the Franchisee commences business or as soon thereafter as is practical. The cost of instruction and related materials for two (2) persons is borne by the Company. All other expenses incurred in connection with the initial training program, including, but not limited to, those for accommodations, travel, and wages of the persons to be trained, are borne by the Franchisee. Either the Franchisee and/or his designee(s) will complete the initial training program to the Company's satisfaction.

2.   <u>Confidential Training/Operations Manual:</u> In order to maintain uniform standards of services, programs, products, and operations offered and sold under the Company's Proprietary Marks (as defined in *Item XIII.*), to promote the goodwill of all Wicks 'N' Sticks stores, and for the mutual benefit of the Company and the Franchisee, the Company loans the Franchisee one (1) copy of the Confidential Training/ Operations Manual to guide the Franchisee in the operation of his franchised business pursuant to Article IV.C., page D-3 of the Franchise Agreement (Exhibit "D"). The subject matter of the Confidential Training/Operations Manual may include, but is not limited to, merchandise presentation, ordering procedures, merchandise receiving,

merchandise administration, register procedures, and staffing and payroll guidelines. The Franchisee will conduct his business in strict compliance with the Company's operational systems, procedures, policies, methods, and requirements as prescribed in the Confidential Training/Operations Manual.

Pre-Opening Assistance: Although not obligated to do so by the Franchise Agreement or any other agreement, prior to the opening of the franchise business, the Company may provide the following assistance:

1.   Site Selection: The Company offers to provide assistance to the Franchisee in screening and selecting a location and negotiating the lease for the operation of the franchised business. The franchise is granted for a specific location. The proposed lease and any other information as the Company may reasonably require will be submitted to the Company for its approval. If the Company does not approve the lease or any other information, the Franchisee is prohibited from opening the franchised business at that location.

2.   Specifications: The Company provides the Franchisee with specifications for all initial equipment, inventory, fixtures, and supplies required in connection with the operation of the franchised business.

3.   Visual Merchandising Plans and Display Materials: The Company may provide a floor plan for the location which may include, but is not limited to, fixture and product layout and store color scheme.

4.   Fixture Layout and Specifications: The Company provides fixture layout and specifications for the build out of the store including, but not limited to, finish materials, color schemes, and store front design.

5.   Employee Training: The Company provides assistance to the Franchisee in training the employees of the franchised business.

6.   Assistance for Veterans: The Company participates in the Veterans Transition Franchise Initiative (VETFRAN) which is a program designed to assist veterans in purchasing a franchised business with reduced capital requirements. In connection therewith, the Company will finance up to fifty percent (50%) of the franchise fee for veterans.

Post-Opening Obligations: During the operation of the franchised business and pursuant to Article IV.D., page D-3 of the Franchise Agreement (Exhibit "D"), the Company is obligated to continue its efforts to maintain high and uniform standards of quality, cleanliness, appearance, and service and to make reasonable efforts to disseminate the Company's standards and specifications to the Franchisee.

Wicks 'N' Sticks Franchise Offering Circular
Effective May 7, 1993.

Post-Opening Assistance: Although not obligated to do so by the Franchise Agreement or any other agreement, during the operation of the franchised business, the Company assists the Franchisee by providing the following:

1.   Additional Training Programs: The Company may offer additional training programs, at which attendance may be mandatory and for which the Company bears the costs of the instruction and required materials. All other expenses incurred in connection with any such additional training programs, including, but not limited to, those for accommodations, travel, and wages, are to be borne by the Franchisee. These training programs may be held at locations designated by the Company. The duration of any such program may vary.

2.   Buying Shows: As of the date of this offering circular, the Company offers two (2) Wicks 'N' Sticks Buying Shows annually which provide Franchisees the opportunity to view and/or to purchase merchandise, fixtures, and services from suppliers who have been approved by the Company. Additionally, the Company may conduct workshops where the Company's personnel and/or guest speakers provide direction and guidance in various facets of the Franchisee's business.

3.   Area Meetings: Field personnel may periodically conduct area meetings to exchange ideas on a local level.

4.   R.A.W. Program: The Royalties At Work ("R.A.W.") Program specializes in topics in the merchandising, operations, marketing, and small business management areas. Information is introduced through a unique binder system and through field training classes presented by employees of the Company.

5.   On-going Field Support: The Company provides on-going support in areas of merchandising, training, and store management.

6.   Negotiations with Approved Suppliers: The Company conducts negotiations with certain suppliers to secure quality products and services as well as favorable pricing.

7.   Negotiations With Freight Companies: The Company conducts negotiations with certain freight companies to secure favorable rates.

8.   Awards Program: The Company conducts an on-going Awards Program for Franchisees. The awards are primarily based on a Franchisee's percentage of increase over the previous year's sales and on the total sales volume of his franchised business. Additional incentive programs may occasionally be offered.

Wicks 'N' Sticks Franchise Offering Circular
Effective May 7, 1993.

9.   Discovery Line: The Company provides a toll-free number for Franchisees to enable them to obtain and/or share product and supplier information related to new product lines, trend updates, and vendor inquiries.

Commencement of Operations Subsequent to the Signing of the Franchise Agreement: The length of time between the signing of the Franchise Agreement and the opening of the Franchisee's business depends upon the type of store the Franchisee is purchasing. In the case of an existing Company-owned store, the length of time is usually between two (2) and eight (8) weeks. In the case of a new store, the length of time varies considerably due in part to the time required to negotiate the lease, prepare plans and specifications, acquire financing, obtain construction bids, build the store, order and set up the fixtures, and display the merchandise. Thus, the length of time between the signing of the Franchise Agreement and the opening of a new store usually ranges from three (3) to twelve (12) months. In either case, the ability of the Franchisee to obtain any necessary financing may also affect the amount of time between the signing of the Franchise Agreement and the opening of the business.

NO OTHER SUPERVISION, ASSISTANCE, OR SERVICES ARE PROVIDED BY THE COMPANY IN CONNECTION WITH THE ESTABLISHMENT OR OPERATION OF THE FRANCHISED BUSINESS.

ITEM XII

EXCLUSIVE AREA OR TERRITORY

Territorial Rights and Obligations: Provided the Franchisee has timely met all of his obligations under the Franchise Agreement and all other agreements with the Company, the Company agrees not to locate, operate, or cause to be located or operated another Wicks 'N' Sticks store within the same mall as the franchised business. A prospective franchisee may be offered a Franchise Option Agreement (Exhibit "F"), which grants him the opportunity to purchase a Wicks 'N' Sticks store within a designated territory within a specified time period.

The Franchise Option Agreement may only be modified by written instrument signed by both parties.

Wicks 'N' Sticks Franchise Offering Circular
Effective May 7, 1993.

ITEM XIII

TRADEMARKS, SERVICE MARKS, TRADE NAMES, LOGOTYPES, AND COMMERCIAL SYMBOLS

Under the Franchise Agreement, the Franchisees are licensed to use only the Company's mark "Wicks 'N' Sticks" and such other trade names, service marks, and trademarks as are now or are hereafter designated by the Company as part of the System (hereinafter referred to as "Proprietary Marks") only in connection with the operation of the licensed business.

The Company has registered the following trademarks, service marks, trade names, logotypes, or other commercial symbols listed below on the federal level with the United States Patent and Trademark Office on the Principal Register:

> Wicks 'N' Sticks (service mark)
> Registration No. 1,148,315
> Registered March 10, 1981
>
> Wicks 'N' Sticks (trademark)
> Registration No. 1,181,785
> Registered December 15, 1981

All affidavits of use required to be filed to maintain the registration of the marks have been timely filed. The Wicks 'N' Sticks marks have become incontestable. The Company has common law rights with respect to the mark based on first use in trade in addition to the registration mentioned above. The Proprietary Marks are not registered in this State.

Wicks 'N' Sticks Franchise Offering Circular
Effective May 7, 1993.

There are no presently effective determinations of the patent office, the trademark administrator of this State or any court, or any pending interference, opposition, or cancellation proceeding, or any pending material litigation involving Proprietary Marks which are relevant to their use in this State or in any other state in which the franchised business is to be located.

As of the date of this offering circular, there are no agreements in effect which significantly limit the rights of the Company to use or license the use of such Proprietary Marks in any manner material to the franchise. Although the Company is not obligated to protect the rights which the Franchisee has to use such Proprietary Marks or to protect the Franchisee against claims of infringement and unfair competition, it has been the Company's policy to do so in the past.

The Franchisee is obligated to promptly notify the Company of his knowledge of any actual, possible, or potential unauthorized use of the Proprietary Marks (or any colorable variation thereof), or of any other name, mark, or symbol in which the Company claims a proprietary interest or which is confusingly similar thereto. The Franchisee is obligated to promptly notify the Company of any litigation instituted against the Franchisee involving allegations of unauthorized use of the Proprietary Marks. Within ten (10) days of receipt of such notice, the Company will notify the Franchisee of its election to either defend and assume control of such litigation or to decline to defend and assume control of such litigation. The Company is not obligated to defend the Franchisee against any third party claim that the Franchisee's operation of the licensed business or the Franchisee's use of the Proprietary Marks infringes any right of such third party and the Company is not obligated to protect, indemnify, or hold harmless the Franchisee from the consequences of any such claim or litigation. If the Company defends and assumes control of such litigation, the Company may, without the Franchisee's consent, settle or compromise any such claims on such terms as the Company, in its sole discretion, may deem appropriate provided that any monetary settlement entered into without the Franchisee's consent is to be paid by the Company. If the Company declines to defend and assume control of such litigation, the Franchisee may not settle or otherwise compromise any such claim without the Company's prior approval thereof. The Franchise Agreement grants the Company the right to control any administrative proceedings or litigation relating to the Proprietary Marks. The Franchisee is required to execute all documents requested by the Company or its counsel that are necessary to obtain protection for the Proprietary Marks or to maintain their continued validity or enforceability and to take no action that would jeopardize the validity or enforceability of such Proprietary Marks.

Wicks 'N' Sticks Uniform Franchise Offering Circular
Effective May 7, 1993.

Under the Franchise Agreement, the Franchisee agrees not to contest, directly or indirectly, the Company's ownership, title, right, or interest in its names or marks, trade secrets, methods, procedures, and advertising techniques which are part of the Company's business or contest the Company's sole right to register, use, or license others to use such names and marks, trade secrets, methods, procedures, and techniques. Upon expiration or termination of the Franchise Agreement, the Company has the right to require the Franchisee to discontinue the use of the name Wicks 'N' Sticks, any other Proprietary Marks of the Company, or any mark or name similar thereto.

There are no infringing uses actually known to the Company that could materially affect the Franchisee's use of such trademark, service mark, trade name, logotype, or other commercial symbol in this State or any other state in which the franchised business is to be located.

ITEM XIV

PATENTS AND COPYRIGHTS

Proprietary Rights: The Company does not own any patents or copyrights that are material to the franchise. However, the Company does own all proprietary rights in and to the System. The Franchise Agreement provides that the Franchisee acknowledges that his entire knowledge of the System, the contents of the Confidential Training/Operations Manual, and all other information, knowledge, and know-how designated by the Company is confidential, is derived from information disclosed to the Franchisee by the Company pursuant to the Franchise Agreement, and that such information is proprietary and confidential, and may be a trade secret of the Company. The Franchise Agreement further provides that the Franchisee will:

1.   Refrain from using any of the Proprietary Marks, or any part or form thereof, in conjunction with any other work or symbol without the Company's prior written consent;

2.   Refrain from selling to another retailer, discounter, or other entity that intends to resell products which bear the Proprietary Marks;

3.   Feature and use the Proprietary Marks solely in the manner prescribed by the Company;

Wicks 'N' Sticks Uniform Franchise Offering Circular
Effective May 7, 1993.

4.   Refrain from manufacturing, reproducing, reprinting, or causing to be manufactured, reproduced, or reprinted, any of the Proprietary Marks, or any part or form thereof, without the Company's prior written consent;

5.   Observe all such requirements with respect to trademark, service mark, and copyright notices, fictitious name registrations, and the display of the legal name or other identification of the Franchisee as the Company may direct in writing from time to time; and

6.   Use, promote, and offer for sale under the Proprietary Marks only those products and service which meet the Company's prescribed standards and specifications, as they may be revised and amended by the Company from time to time.

The Franchisee, his employees, agents, and representatives will:

1.   At all times treat the Confidential Training/Operations Manual, any other manuals created or approved for use in the operation of the licensed business, and the information contained therein, as confidential, proprietary information of the Company disclosed to the Franchisee under an agreement of confidentiality;

2.   Use all reasonable efforts to maintain such information as secret and confidential; and

3.   Not copy, duplicate, record, or otherwise reproduce the Confidential Training/Operations Manual (in whole or in part) nor otherwise make the standards or procedures disclosed to the Franchisee by the Company available to any unauthorized person without the Company's prior written consent.

The Franchise Agreement prohibits the Franchisee from communicating, divulging, or using any such confidential and/or trade secret information for the benefit of any other person or legal entity and requires the Franchisee to use all reasonable efforts to maintain the confidentiality and/or secrecy of such information at all times during and after the term of the Franchise Agreement.

Wicks 'N' Sticks Uniform Franchise Offering Circular
Effective May 7, 1993.

ITEM XV

OBLIGATION OF THE FRANCHISEE TO PARTICIPATE IN THE ACTUAL OPERATION OF THE FRANCHISED BUSINESS

The Company's experience has shown that Franchisees who participate directly in the operation of the franchised business increase the likelihood of better overall performance. Therefore, the Company requires the Franchisee to participate personally in the direct operation of the franchised business and requires him or his designated manager to devote full time, energy, and effort to the management and operation of such business.

ITEM XVI

RESTRICTION ON GOODS AND SERVICES OFFERED BY THE FRANCHISEE

The Franchisee may use the premises only for the retail sale of candles, candle accessories, room fragrances, room fragrance accessories, wedding and special occasion keepsakes, and other related decorative accessories and services. The Franchisee is prohibited from offering or selling any products or services not authorized by the Company and from using the premises for any other purpose than the operation of a Wicks 'N' Sticks store. The Franchisee is not restricted as to the customers to whom he may sell such goods and services. See the prior disclosure under *Item IX*.

ITEM XVII

RENEWAL, TERMINATION, REPURCHASE, MODIFICATION AND ASSIGNMENT OF THE FRANCHISE AGREEMENT, AND RELATED INFORMATION

Initial Term of The Franchise: The initial term of the franchise is usually for a period of ten (10) years from the date of the opening of the Franchisee's Wicks 'N' Sticks store or for the term of the lease, whichever is shorter. The term of the franchise is only affected by the Franchise Agreement and the lease.

Renewal of the Franchise: The Franchise Agreement provides for renewal of the franchise for four (4) separate and successive terms of five (5) years each; provided, however, that such renewal terms will not extend beyond the remaining term of the lease for the franchised business including all renewal terms of such lease. To renew the franchise,

Wicks 'N' Sticks Uniform Franchise Offering Circular
Effective May 7, 1993.

the Franchisee will provide the Company with a written request for renewal for each term not less than nine (9) months, nor more than twelve (12) months, prior to the expiration of the then-current term of the Franchise Agreement. The Company will not unreasonably withhold its approval of such request but may condition its approval upon whether the Franchisee has fully and timely satisfied all obligations owed to the Company and the Lessor and is not otherwise in default of any agreement with the Company or the Lessor.

Upon approval of the Franchisee's request for renewal, the Franchisee will be required to:

1.   Execute the Company's then-current franchise agreement which may contain terms and conditions substantially different from those set forth herein, including, but not limited to, the then-current rate for royalties, advertising, and other payments as such franchise agreement may provide. However, the Franchisee shall not be required to pay any additional initial franchise fee;

2.   Execute a General Release under seal, in a form satisfactory to the Company, releasing any and all claims he may have against the Company and its officers, directors, shareholders, and employees, in their corporate and individual capacities, including, but not limited to, all claims arising under any federal, state, or local law, rule, or ordinance. If the state law prohibits the giving of a General Release at the time of renewal of the franchise, then the execution of a General Release shall not be required. If a release of some, but not all, claims is permitted, the Franchisee shall execute a release to the extent permitted; and

3.   Remodel the premises of the franchised business, including, but not limited to, renovating and modernizing the layout, sign, equipment, furnishings, and decor to reflect the then-current store appearance as required by the Company.

In the event the Franchisee does not satisfactorily comply with the requirements for renewal, the Company has the right to refuse to renew or extend the term of the franchise. The determination as to such unsatisfactory compliance is in the sole discretion of the Company. The Company is not obligated to provide the Franchisee with prior notification of its refusal to renew or extend the Franchise Agreement. Any dispute regarding renewal is to be resolved in accordance with the provisions of Article XXII. of the Franchise Agreement.

Relocation of the Franchise: In the event the Franchisee has not had the opportunity to operate the store at the franchised location for the initial term of the Franchise Agreement due to expiration or termination of the lease, or if the premises is damaged,

Wicks 'N' Sticks Uniform Franchise Offering Circular
Effective May 7, 1993.

condemned, or otherwise rendered unusable, and provided he has fully complied with the terms of the Franchise Agreement, the Franchisee may relocate the franchise to another site if: (1) the site has been approved by the Company in writing (which approval will not be unreasonably withheld); (2) such store is opened within one (1) year from the date the store at the franchised location is closed; and (3) the store appearance of the new location is in accordance with the Company's then-current requirements. If the Franchisee relocates his store to a new site, he may be required to pay to the Company an administrative fee not to exceed twenty percent (20%) of the then-current initial franchise fee. Such administrative fee must be received prior to the effective date of the relocation. Any costs associated with such relocation will be at the Franchisee's expense.

Termination by the Franchisee: The Franchisee has no right to terminate the Franchise Agreement.

Termination by the Company without Notice: The Franchise Agreement and all rights granted therein to the Franchisee automatically terminate without notice to the Franchisee if:

1.   The Franchisee becomes insolvent;

2.   The Franchisee makes a general assignment for the benefit of creditors;

3.   A petition in bankruptcy is filed by the Franchisee or such a petition is filed against or consented to by the Franchisee;

4.   The Franchisee is adjudicated as bankrupt or insolvent;

5.   A bill in equity or other proceeding for the appointment of a receiver of the Franchisee or other custodian for the Franchisee's business or other assets is filed and consented to by the Franchisee;

6.   A receiver or other custodian (permanent or temporary) of the Franchisee's assets, or any part thereof, is appointed by a court of competent jurisdiction;

7.   Proceedings for a composition with creditors under any state or federal law are instituted by or against the Franchisee;

8.   A final judgment for $1,000 or more remains unsatisfied or of record for thirty (30) days or longer (unless supersedeas bond is filed);

9.   Execution is levied against the Franchisee's business or other assets;

Wicks 'N' Sticks Uniform Franchise Offering Circular
Effective May 7, 1993.

10.   Suit to foreclose any lien against the assets of the franchised business is instituted against the Franchisee and not dismissed within thirty (30) days; or

11.   The assets of the franchised business are sold after levy thereupon by any means.

The Franchise Agreement provides for termination upon bankruptcy. This provision may not be enforceable under federal bankruptcy law (11 U.S.C.A. Sec. 101 et seq.).

Termination by the Company with Notice: The Franchise Agreement and all rights granted therein to the Franchisee terminate effective immediately upon the Franchisee's receipt of a Notice of Termination if:

1.   The Franchisee ceases to operate the business licensed by the Franchise Agreement or otherwise abandons the business or forfeits the legal right to transact business at the franchised location;

2.   The Franchisee is convicted of a felony, any crime involving moral turpitude, or any other crime or offense that is reasonably likely, in the sole opinion of the Company, to adversely affect the name or goodwill of the Company, the System, the Proprietary Mark, or the Company's rights therein;

3.   The Franchisee, without the Company's prior written consent, purports to transfer any rights or obligations arising under the Franchise Agreement to any third party including, but not limited to, any unapproved transfer by operation of law;

4.   Upon death or permanent incapacity of any individual Franchisee or a person with a direct controlling interest in the Franchisee (if the Franchisee is a corporation or partnership), his legal representative does not effect a transfer of the decedent's or incapacitated party's interest in the Franchise Agreement with the Company's prior consent within the time required by the Franchise Agreement;

5.   The Franchisee misuses or makes any unauthorized use of the Proprietary Marks, any other identifying characteristics of the System, or otherwise materially impairs the goodwill associated therewith or the Company's rights therein including, but not limited to, failure to comply with the in-term covenants contained in Article XIV. of the Franchise Agreement;

6.   The Franchisee understates gross sales by three percent (3%) or more in any gross sales report or falsely reports any other information to the Company;

7.   The franchised location is used for any unlawful or unauthorized purpose; or

Wicks 'N' Sticks Uniform Franchise Offering Circular
Effective May 7, 1993.

8.   The Franchisee does not purchase or maintain any insurance required by the Franchise Agreement or does not reimburse the Company for its purchase of such insurance on behalf of the Franchisee within thirty (30) days of receipt of an invoice therefor.

9.   The Franchisee's lease is terminated by the Lessor.

Termination by the Company with Notice of Default and Termination: The Franchisee is in default if he does not substantially comply with any of the terms of the Franchise Agreement or to carry out the terms thereof in good faith. Defaults include, but are not limited to, the occurrence of any of the following:

1.   The Franchisee does not provide the Company with a copy of the fully executed lease for the franchised location within ninety (90) days of the date of the Franchise Agreement (if applicable) and/or does not open his store within the time required in the lease for the franchised location;

2.   The Franchisee fails, refuses, or neglects to timely pay any amounts owed to the Company, the Lessor, or any suppliers on or before the date payment is due;

3.   The Franchisee fails, refuses, or neglects to timely submit any required reports to the Company;

4.   The Franchisee fails, refuses, or neglects to obtain the Company's prior written approval of any matter or transaction where such approval is required by the terms of the Franchise Agreement;

5.   The Franchisee or his manager dose not complete any required training programs to the Company's reasonable satisfaction; or

6.   The Franchisee fails, refuses, or neglects to operate the franchised business in accordance with the Company's standards and specifications.

The Franchisee has thirty (30) calendar days after receipt or refusal of a written Notice of Default and Termination from the Company within which to remedy any of the above defaults. If any such default is not cured within said time period, the Franchise Agreement and all rights granted therein will automatically terminate effective upon the expiration of said thirty (30) day period without further notice or action on the part of the Company. A Notice of Termination sent to the Franchisee by the Company does not constitute a modification of the Notice of Default and Termination.

Wicks 'N' Sticks Uniform Franchise Offering Circular
Effective May 7, 1993.

Post-Expiration and Post-Termination Obligations: Upon the expiration or termination of the Franchise Agreement, except for other locations licensed to the Franchisee by the Company, the Franchisee will:

1. Immediately cease to operate the franchised business and will not thereafter, directly or indirectly, represent to the public or hold himself out as a present or former Franchisee of the Company.

2. Immediately cease to use, by advertising or in any other manner whatsoever, the name Wicks 'N' Sticks or any other Proprietary Marks of the Company, any mark or name similar thereto, or any aspect of the trade dress of the System;

3. Immediately cease using any methods, procedures, techniques, systems, or materials of any kind or nature whatsoever which are trade secrets of the Company;

4. Immediately surrender to the Company all documents in his possession or control relating to the franchised business including, but not limited to, manuals, records, files, instructions, correspondence, and any and all other materials (all of which are hereby acknowledged by the Franchisee to be the Company's property). The Franchisee may not retain any copy or record of the foregoing except for a copy of the Franchise Agreement, any correspondence between the parties, and any other documents which the Franchisee reasonably needs to comply with any provision of law. Notwithstanding the foregoing, the Franchisee may be entitled to retain copies of information which do not belong to the Company and/or which do not contain any of the Company's proprietary information;

5. Not remove any inventory, fixtures, or equipment from the franchised location which are subject to any security interest of the Company or any other party;

6. Not remove any inventory, fixtures, or equipment from the franchised location if the Franchisee is still obligated for amounts owed to the Company;

7. Immediately offer to surrender possession of the location to the Company;

8. Transfer and assign to the Company his right, title, and interest to any telephone number and telephone directory listing then or theretofore used in connection with the operation of the franchised business and appoint the Company as his agent and attorney-in-fact to perfect the transfer and assignment of such number and directly listing to the Company or its designee;

9. Immediately pay all amounts owed (including the outstanding principal amounts and accrued interest on any notes or evidences of indebtedness of the

Wicks 'N' Sticks Uniform Franchise Offering Circular
Effective May 7, 1993.

Franchisee) to the Company, its subsidiaries, and affiliates as well as to the Lessor, suppliers, and vendors. All amounts owed to the Company, regardless of kind or method of payment agreed upon, accelerate and become due and payable in full. As security for the payment of all such obligations, the Franchisee grants to the Company a lien and security interest against any and all items of personal property owned by the Franchisee and used in connection with the licensed business;

10. Upon the Company's request, promptly execute assignment or other transfer documentation in the form requested by the Company to transfer to the Company or its designee, the Franchisee's interest in or to the right to use and occupy the location. Upon the failure of the Franchisee to timely execute such documentation, the Franchisee irrevocably appoints the Company as the Franchisee's agent and attorney-in-fact to execute same;

11. Immediately cancel all assumed names, corporate names, business names or styles, or other registrations using name, style, symbol, or mark included within the Proprietary Marks or other marks similar thereto which are owned or which have been taken out or filed by the Franchisee. Upon the failure of the Franchisee to timely cancel all such names and registrations, the Franchisee irrevocably appoints the Company as his agent and attorney-in-fact to obtain all such cancellations; and

12. Comply with the post-expiration and post-termination covenants contained in Article XIV. of the Franchise Agreement.

Upon expiration or termination of the Franchise Agreement, and without being liable for trespass, tort, criminal act, or otherwise, in addition to any other rights or remedies available to the Company, it has the right, but not the obligation, to:

1. Enter, inspect, and take control of the franchised business.

2. Remove from the premises of such franchised business all inventory, equipment, supplies, signs, and other materials of any kind or nature whatsoever bearing the Company's Proprietary Marks to prevent the premises of the franchised business from appearing thereafter to be a business premises affiliated with the Company or the System. The cost of such removal will be borne by the Franchisee.

If the Franchisee does not perform any obligation incident to expiration or termination of the Franchise Agreement and the Company proceeds to enforce such obligation, the Franchisee will pay all damages, costs, interest, and expenses incurred by the Company in connection therewith, including actual attorneys' fees and other expenses related to the collection process. Any security interest granted to the

Wicks 'N' Sticks Uniform Franchise Offering Circular
Effective May 7, 1993.

Company by the Franchisee herein will remain in full force and effect until all such obligations, including the costs of enforcement thereof, are fully paid.

Any failure to comply with the requirements of Article XIII. of the Franchise Agreement will cause the Company irreparable injury and the Franchisee hereby consents to the entry of an ex parte order by any court of competent jurisdiction for injunctive or other legal or equitable relief, including an order authorizing the Company, its designees, or agents to enter the premises of the franchised business and to take such action as may be necessary or appropriate to protect the Company's rights.

The Company's Right of First Refusal to Purchase the Franchised Business from the Franchisee: Any party holding any interest in the Franchise Agreement or in the franchised business who desires to accept any bona fide offer to purchase that interest from a third party will notify the Company in writing of such offer, which will include a complete copy of the proposed agreement of sale and all ancillary agreements and documents. The Company has the right and option, exercisable within thirty (30) days from receipt of such documentation, to send written notice to the Franchisee that the Company or its nominee intends to purchase the Franchisee's interest on the same terms and conditions as those offered by the third party. The Company is not obligated to purchase assets which are not directly related to the operation of the franchised business. Such non-related assets are assigned a value by the Company and are deducted from the purchase price offered by the third party. Any dispute concerning the identification or value of non-related assets will not delay the purchase of such assets at the Company's price. Any such dispute will be resolved in accordance with the provisions of Article XXII. of the Franchise Agreement. Any material change in the terms of any offer prior to such purchase constitutes a new offer subject to the same rights of first refusal by the Company or its nominee as in the case of an initial offer. The failure of the Company to exercise such right of first refusal does not constitute a waiver of any other provision of the Franchise Agreement, including, but not limited to, all of the requirements contained in Article XI. of the Franchise Agreement with respect to any proposed transfer.

The Franchisee's Interest Upon Termination or Nonrenewal: The Franchise Agreement contains no provision granting the Franchisee any equity upon termination nor the right to receive any payment or adjustment whatsoever for any goodwill the Franchisee may have established either prior to or during his operation of the franchised business.

Wicks 'N' Sticks Uniform Franchise Offering Circular
Effective May 7, 1993.

The Company's Right to Purchase the Franchise: Upon expiration or termination of the Franchise Agreement and upon thirty (30) days written notice, the Company has the right, but not the obligation, to purchase any or all of the Franchisee's leasehold improvements, fixtures, and equipment at the Franchisee's then-book value, and the Company approved inventory in good and saleable condition at a price not to exceed the Franchisee's cost thereof. The valuation of goodwill is not a factor in the determination of the purchase price. In the event of any dispute regarding the price to be paid, the Company will proceed with such purchase at the price described above. Any dispute regarding price will be resolved in accordance with the provisions of Article XXII. of the Franchise Agreement. Any amounts owed to the Company by the Franchisee are deducted from any amounts owed to the Franchisee by the Company pursuant to said purchase.

Sale, Transfer, or Assignment by the Franchisee: If the Franchisee desires to sell or transfer all or any part of his interest in the Franchise Agreement to any purchaser or transferee, the Franchisee will first obtain the Company's written consent thereto and:

1.   All obligations owed to the Company and all other outstanding obligations relating to the franchised business will be fully paid and satisfied prior to such sale or transfer.

2.   Unless prohibited by the law of the state where the franchised business is located, the Franchisee will execute a General Release under seal, in a form satisfactory to the Company, releasing any and all claims he may have against the Company and its officers, directors, shareholders, and employees in their corporate and individual capacities, including, but not limited to, all claims arising under any federal, state, or local law, rule, or ordinance and any other matters incident to the termination of the Franchise Agreement, the transfer of the Franchisee's interest therein, and the transfer of the Franchisee's ownership of all or any part of the franchised business. If a General Release is prohibited, the Franchisee will execute a release to the extent allowed by law.

3.   The transferee will demonstrate that he satisfies the Company's management, business, and financial standards and otherwise possesses the character and capabilities (including business reputation and credit rating) as the Company may require to conduct the franchised business.

4.   At the Company's option, the transferee and all persons owning any interest in the transferee, will execute the Company's then-current franchise agreement which may contain terms and conditions substantially different from those set forth in the Franchisee's Franchise Agreement.

Wicks 'N' Sticks Uniform Franchise Offering Circular
Effective May 7, 1993.

5.   The transferee will execute a General Release under seal, in a form satisfactory to the Company, releasing any and all claims he may have against the Company and its officers, directors, shareholders, and employees in their corporate and individual capacities, with respect to any representations regarding the franchise, the business conducted pursuant thereto, or any other matter that may have been made to the transferee by the selling Franchisee.

6.   The Franchisee will provide the Company with a complete copy of all contracts, agreements, and related documentation between the Franchisee and the transferee relating to the sale or transfer of the franchised business.

7.   The Franchisee will pay to the Company a transfer fee not to exceed twenty percent (20%) of the then-current initial franchise fee.

8.   If so requested by the Company, the Franchisee shall agree to continue to be bound by the obligations of the new franchise agreement and to guarantee the full performance thereof by the transferee.

Upon the death or incapacity of the Franchisee, the franchised business may be transferred to the Franchisee's heirs or legatees as described in more detail below under the heading *"Rights of the Franchisee's Heirs Upon Death or Incapacity of the Franchisee."*

The Company's consent to a transfer of any interest in the Franchise Agreement or of any ownership interest in the franchised business does not constitute a waiver of any claims the Company may have against the Franchisee or the transferee, nor is it deemed a waiver of the Company's right to demand compliance with the terms of the Franchise Agreement.

Assignment to the Individual Franchisee's Corporation: If the Franchisee desires to assign the Franchise Agreement or any interest therein to a corporation, which is entirely owned by the Franchisee and is being formed for the financial planning, tax, or other convenience of the Franchisee, the Franchisee will first obtain the Company's written consent thereto and:

1.   The Franchisee's corporation will be newly organized and its charter will provide that its activities are confined exclusively to the operation of the franchised business.

2.   The Franchisee will retain total ownership of the outstanding stock or other capital interest in the corporate assignee and will act as the principal officer(s) and director(s) thereof.

Wicks 'N' Sticks Uniform Franchise Offering Circular
Effective May 7, 1993.

3.   All obligations of the Franchisee owed to the Company, the Lessor, and suppliers will be fully paid and satisfied.

4.   The corporate assignee will enter into a written agreement with the Company expressly assuming the obligations of the Franchise Agreement and all other agreements relating to the operation of the franchised business and the use and occupancy of the franchised location. If the consent of any other contracting party to any such agreement is required, the Franchisee will obtain such written consent and provide the same to the Company.

5.   All owners of the stock or other ownership interest of the corporate assignee will enter into an agreement with the Company, jointly and severally guaranteeing the full payment of the corporation's obligations to the Company and the performance by the corporation of all the obligations under the Franchise Agreement, the lease, and/or the Sublease Agreement.

6.   Each stock certificate or other ownership interest certificate of the corporate assignee will have conspicuously endorsed on the face thereof a statement in a form satisfactory to the Company that it is held subject to, and that further assignment or transfer thereof is subject to, all restrictions imposed upon transfers and assignments by the Franchise Agreement.

7.   Copies of the corporate assignee's Articles of Incorporation, Bylaws, and other governing regulations or documents, including resolutions of the Board of Directors authorizing entry into the Franchise Agreement, will be promptly furnished to the Company. Copies of any amendment to any of the above documents will also be furnished to the Company.

8.   The term of the assigned Franchise Agreement is the unexpired term of the franchise.

No transfer fee is charged in connection with such assignment to the Franchisee's corporation.

Assignment by the Company: The Franchise Agreement is fully assignable by the Company and inures to the benefit of any assignee or other legal successor to the interest of the Company.

Modification of the Franchise Agreement: The Franchise Agreement may be modified by a written instrument between the Company and the Franchisee. The Company also reserves the right, from time to time, to amend the contents of the Confidential

Wicks 'N' Sticks Uniform Franchise Offering Circular
Effective May 7, 1993.

Training/Operations Manual and the Franchisee will comply with any new or changed standard or requirement.

Rights of The Franchisee's Heirs Upon Death or Incapacity of the Franchisee: In the event of death or permanent incapacity of any person with an ownership interest in the Franchise Agreement, the decedent's or incapacitated person's rights, title, and interest in and to the Franchise Agreement may pass by Will, Intestate Succession, or Conservatorship, as appropriate, provided that the franchised business is operated in accordance with the provisions of the Franchise Agreement during any period of probate, administration, or guardianship. Should the heirs, legatees, or other persons holding an interest subject to the restrictions of Article XI.I. of the Franchise Agreement be unable to obtain the Company's approval of a transfer of any interest which they would otherwise have received, within ninety (90) days of such death or incapacity, the executor, administrator, guardian, or other personal representative will sell such interest to a transferee acceptable to the Company within six (6) months from the date of notice of the Company's disapproval. The failure to accomplish such sale(s) constitutes a default of the Franchise Agreement giving the Company the right to terminate the Franchise Agreement upon thirty (30) days written notice.

Any transfer by Will, Intestate Succession, or other legal process of the decedent's interest therein by the executor, administrator, guardian, or personal representative of the decedent's estate is considered to be a transfer requiring compliance with the conditions set forth in Article XI. of the Franchise Agreement, except that no transfer fee is charged in the event the decedent's interest passes to an heir named in such a person's Will.

Covenants Not To Compete: During the term of the Franchise Agreement, the Franchisee covenants that neither he nor any person owning at least a five percent (5%) equity interest in the business will:

1.   Either directly or indirectly engage in any other business which offers or sells candles, candle accessories, room fragrances, room fragrance accessories, wedding and special occasion keepsakes, and/or other related decorative accessories and/or services or engage in any of the activities which the Franchise Agreement contemplates will be engaged in by the Franchisee, or offer or sell any other service or product (or component thereof) which comprises or may in the future comprise a part of the franchised system (or any product or service confusingly similar thereto) either as a proprietor, partner, investor, shareholder, director, officer, employee, principal, agent, advisor, or consultant nor divert any business to any other entity that would normally be handled by the franchised business; nor

Wicks 'N' Sticks Uniform Franchise Offering Circular
Effective May 7, 1993.

2.   Hire personnel of the Company or its parent (or the subsidiaries, affiliates, or designees of either entity) or of any other Franchisee of the Company.

For a period of two (2) years after expiration or termination of the Franchise Agreement, the Franchisee covenants that neither he nor any person owning at least a five percent (5%) equity interest in the business will:

1.   Within a ten (10) mile radius of the franchised location or within a ten (10) mile radius of any existing Wicks 'N' Sticks store either directly or indirectly engage in any other business which offers or sells candles, candle accessories, room fragrances, room fragrance accessories, wedding and special occasion keepsakes, and/or other related decorative accessories and/or services or engage in any of the activities which the Franchise Agreement contemplates will be engaged in by the Franchisee, or offer or sell any other service or product (or component thereof) which comprises or may in the future comprise a part of the franchised system (or any product or service confusingly similar thereto) either as a proprietor, partner, investor, shareholder, director, officer, employee, principal, agent, advisor, or consultant nor divert any business to any other entity that would normally be handled by the franchised business; nor

2.   Hire personnel of the Company or its parent (or the subsidiaries, affiliates, or designees of either entity) or of any other Franchisee of the Company.

This precludes not only direct competition but also all forms of indirect competition, such as consultation for competitive businesses, service as an independent contractor for such competitive businesses, or any assistance or disclosure of information of any kind or nature whatsoever which would be of any material assistance to a competitor. Nothing prevents the Franchisee from owning for investment purposes up to an aggregate of five percent (5%) of the capital stock of any such competitive business, provided that said business is a publicly held corporation whose stock is listed and traded on a national or regional stock exchange or through the National Association of Securities Dealers Automated Quotation System (NASDAQ), and provided that the Franchisee does not control any such company.

The time periods for the post-expiration and post-termination covenants contained in Article XIV. of the Franchise Agreement are tolled and do not run during any period of noncompliance by the Franchisee. The time period of each such covenant is extended to include all periods of noncompliance therewith.

Wicks 'N' Sticks Uniform Franchise Offering Circular
Effective May 7, 1993.

Dispute Resolution: Article XXII. of the Franchise Agreement provides that in the event of any dispute between the Company and the Franchisee (except for any dispute relating to monies owed, trademark infringement, default under the Franchise Agreement, termination of the Franchise Agreement, covenants upon termination or expiration of the Franchise Agreement, any lease an/or sublease agreement, or as otherwise specifically provided in the Franchise Agreement) whether or not arising out of the Franchise Agreement or any other agreement between the Company and the Franchisee whether entered into prior, on, or subsequent to the date of the Franchise Agreement, the Company and the Franchisee will, prior to instituting any litigation, endeavor to resolve any such dispute in accordance with the alternative dispute resolution process ("ADR Process") as provided therein. Any litigation between the Company and the Franchisee may only be brought in the United States District Court for the district nearest the then-current home office of the Company, provided federal jurisdiction is obtainable, and in the event federal jurisdiction is not obtainable, in the local state court in the country in which the home office of the Company is then located. Except as otherwise provided in the Franchise Agreement, the Franchise Agreement shall be interpreted, governed, and construed pursuant to the laws of the State of Texas and such laws shall prevail in the event of any conflict of law unless the application of Texas law would render the Franchise Agreement or a particular portion of the Franchise Agreement (e.g., the forum selection clause) unenforceable, in which case the laws of the state where the franchised business is located shall be applied if the application of such laws would render the Franchise Agreement or such portion thereof enforceable. Notwithstanding the ADR Process, the Company may proceed directly to court in whatever forum the Company deems appropriate to obtain injunctive relief against conduct (threatened or otherwise) that may cause the Company loss or damage. The provisions of Article XXII. of the Franchise Agreement also apply to any such dispute between the Company, the Company's officers, directors, shareholders, representatives, agents, or employees, on the one hand, and the Franchisee, the Franchisee's officers, directors, shareholders, representatives, agents, or employees, on the other hand, whether or not any of such individuals are parties to the Franchise Agreement. The Company reserves the right, in its sole discretion, to unilaterally delete from the Franchise Agreement the obligation to submit any dispute to the ADR Process upon giving thirty (30) days written notice to the Franchisee. The Franchisee should refer to Articles XXI. and XXII. of the Franchise Agreement regarding these matters.

Wicks 'N' Sticks Uniform Franchise Offering Circular
Effective May 7, 1993.

ITEM XVIII

ARRANGEMENTS WITH PUBLIC FIGURES

No compensation or other benefit is given or promised to public figures arising, in whole or in part, from the use of a public figure in the name or symbol of the franchise, or the endorsement or recommendation of the franchise by a public figure in advertisements. The Franchisee does not have a right to use the name of a public figure in his own promotional efforts or advertising, but the Company will consider written requests for permission to conduct such advertising in accordance with its right or prior approval of all advertising by the Franchisee. There are no public figures involved in the actual management or control of the Company.

ITEM XIX

REPRESENTATIONS REGARDING EARNINGS CAPABILITY

Except as described below, the Company does not furnish or authorize its salespersons to furnish any oral or written information concerning the actual or potential sales, costs, income or profits of the Wicks 'N' Sticks stores. Actual results vary from unit to unit and the Company cannot estimate the results of any particular franchise.

At the end of the calendar year 1992, there were One hundred ninety-eight (198) Wicks 'N' Sticks stores. The sales figures included in the Statement of Average Sales and Expenses ("Statement") included as part of this *Item XIX* are for the calendar year 1992 and are based upon one hundred seventy-seven (177) franchised Wicks 'N' Sticks stores which were in operation for the entire calendar years 1991 and 1992. Twelve (12) stores were not included in the Statement because they were not operated as franchised or changed ownership during the calendar years 1991 and 1992. Five (5) stores were not included because the franchisee did not report the full year's gross sales to the Company. Three (3) stores were not included because they were operated as Company-owned stores. One (1) store was not included because it was closed for a part of the calendar year 1992.

The information included in the Statement was obtained from a survey which was sent to the Wicks 'N' Sticks stores. The expense figures included in the Statement are for the calendar year 1992 and are based upon fifty-nine (59) franchised Wicks 'N' Sticks stores which were in operation for the entire calendar years 1991 and 1992. Other than the twenty-one (21) stores not included that were mentioned above, one hundred eighteen (118) stores were not included in the Statement because the Franchisees did not respond to the survey.

Wicks 'N' Sticks Uniform Franchise Offering Circular
Effective May 7, 1993.

Except where otherwise noted, the following data was compiled from sales and expense information reported to the Company by the Franchisees of such stores. Although the Franchise Agreement requires the Franchisee to maintain records in accordance with generally accepted accounting principles, the Company provides no assurance that such records were maintained in accordance therewith. The numbers actually reported to the Company by the Franchisees may vary from those numbers reported on each Franchisee's individual financial statements due to different reporting periods, different accounting methods, and different reasons for preparation, i.e., tax purposes. Therefore, no reconciliation of these numbers to the individual financial statements is available to the Company. A Franchisee may have additional expenses which are not included in the Statement. The fifty-nine (59) stores included in the Statement did not receive any services which were not generally available to other franchised stores. Each store offered similar products and services as would generally be offered by a typical new franchised store.

A NEW FRANCHISEE'S INDIVIDUAL FINANCIAL RESULTS ARE LIKELY TO DIFFER FROM THE RESULTS STATED IN THE STATEMENT.

Wicks 'N' Sticks Uniform Franchise Offering Circular
Effective May 7, 1993.

THESE SALES, PROFITS, OR EARNINGS ARE AVERAGE OF SPECIFIC FRANCHISEES AND SHOULD NOT BE CONSIDERED AS THE ACTUAL OR POTENTIAL SALES, PROFITS, OR EARNINGS THAT WILL BE REALIZED BY ANY OTHER FRANCHISEE. THE COMPANY DOES NOT REPRESENT THAT ANY FRANCHISEE CAN EXPECT TO ATTAIN THESE SALES, PROFITS, OR EARNINGS. A NEW FRANCHISEE'S INDIVIDUAL FINANCIAL RESULTS ARE LIKELY TO DIFFER FROM THOSE BELOW. NO PERSON HAS ANY AUTHORITY TO MAKE ANY REPRESENTATION THAT ANY LEVEL OF SALES OR PROFITS WILL BE ACHIEVED BY ANY FRANCHISEE.

WICKS 'N' STICKS
STATEMENT OF AVERAGE SALES AND EXPENSES
(NATIONAL)

Sales (a)	$315,962
Cost Of Goods Sold (b)	134,472
Gross Margin	$181,489

Operating Expenses

Employee Expenses (c)	32,864
Supplies (d)	3,758
Advertising (e)	2,841
Royalties (f)	18,958
Minimum Rent and Other Lease Charges (g)	35,463
Occupancy Charges (h)	8,297
Miscellaneous (i)	21,400
Total Operating Expenses	123,581

Net Income Before Interest, Depreciation, Debt Service and Taxes	$57,908

Notes:

(a)   Sales — This figure represents the average gross sales as reported for the full calendar year 1992 for the one hundred seventy-seven (177) franchised stores described above.

(b)   Cost Of Goods Sold — This figure was calculated based upon the percentage of the average cost of goods sold (42.58%) reported by the owners of fifty-nine (59) stores. This figure may be affected by factors including, but not limited to, shrinkage, markdowns, associate discounts, and outgoing freight charges.

Wicks 'N' Sticks Uniform Franchise Offering Circular
Effective May 7, 1993.

(c)   Employee Expenses — This figure represents the average employee expenses (not including the store manager's salary) reported by the Franchisees of fifty-nine (59) stores. Of the fifty-nine (59) stores reporting employee expenses, twenty-four (24) stores reported amounts over the average range shown above.

(d)   Supplies — This figure represents the average cost of supplies reported by the Franchisees of fifty-six (56) stores. Franchisees from three (3) stores did not provide information on supplies. Of the fifty-six (56) reporting supplies, twenty-two (22) stores reported amounts over the average range.

(e)   Advertising — This figure represents the average expenditure for advertising reported by the Franchisees of fifty-seven (57) stores. Franchisees from two (2) stores did not provide information on advertising. Of the fifty-seven (57) stores reporting advertising, eighteen (18) reported amounts over the average range.

(f)   Royalties — This figure was calculated based upon the Company's current royalty fee of six percent (6%) of gross sales as disclosed in *Item VI* hereof.

(g)   Minimum Rent and Other Lease Charges — This figure represents the average annual minimum rent plus percentage rent, if any, for fifty-nine (59) stores. Of the fifty-nine (59) stores reporting, twenty-three (23) reported amounts over the average range.

(h)   Occupancy Charges — This could include CAM, security, trash removal, Merchant's Association dues, mall promotional expenses and real estate taxes. This figure represents the average occupancy charges of forty-nine (49) stores. Franchises from ten (10) stores did not report occupancy charges. Of the forty-nine stores reporting, twenty-one (21) reported amounts over the average range for occupancy charges.

(i)   Other Expenses — This category comprises all other expense items not previously considered elsewhere in this Statement and would include such items as business insurance, credit card charges, dues and subscriptions, promotional fees, supplies, travel/entertainment, donations, bad debts, bank service charges, interest expense, repairs, postage, property taxes (not paid with "Minimum Rent and Occupancy Charges"), but does not include expenses related to amortization, depreciation or leasehold interest. The figure shown is the average annual expense of fifty-nine (59) stores. Of the fifty-nine (59) stores reporting other expenses, fifteen (15) were over the average range.

The highest and lowest annual sales volumes in 1992 for these Wicks 'N' Sticks stores were $677,497 and $118,034 respectively.

Wicks 'N' Sticks Uniform Franchise Offering Circular
Effective May 7, 1993.

SUBSTANTIATION OF INFORMATION CONTAINED HEREIN WILL BE MADE AVAILABLE TO PROSPECTIVE FRANCHISEES AT THE COMPANY'S HEADQUARTERS UPON REASONABLE DEMAND.

THESE SALES, PROFITS, OR EARNINGS ARE AVERAGES OF SPECIFIC FRANCHISEES AND SHOULD NOT BE CONSIDERED AS THE ACTUAL OR POTENTIAL SALES, PROFITS, OR EARNINGS THAT WILL BE REALIZED BY ANY OTHER FRANCHISEE. THE COMPANY DOES NOT REPRESENT THAT ANY FRANCHISEE CAN EXPECT TO ATTAIN THESE SALES, PROFITS, OR EARNINGS. A NEW FRANCHISEE'S INDIVIDUAL FINANCIAL RESULTS ARE LIKELY TO DIFFER FROM THOSE ABOVE. NO PERSON HAS ANY AUTHORITY TO MAKE ANY REPRESENTATION THAT ANY LEVEL OF SALES OR PROFITS WILL BE ACHIEVED BY ANY FRANCHISEE.

Investment Considerations: Unlike investments where money is earned through the efforts of others, a franchise requires that a Franchisee effectively devote his time and skill to the management of the business. The quality and quantity of the Franchisee's efforts are ultimately reflected in the profits and losses of the business.

The Franchise Agreement and related agreements, such as a lease or sublease, are generally for a term of ten (10) years. If the Franchisee decides that he no longer wishes to operate the franchised business, it is the Franchisee's responsibility to find an acceptable purchaser.

Many factors (which change from time to time) may affect the franchised business during the term of the franchise. These factors include, but are not limited to, the demographics of the area, competition in the area, accessibility and visibility of the location, other economic conditions of the market place, and the Franchisee's continuing commitment to the franchised business.

Wicks 'N' Sticks Uniform Franchise Offering Circular
Effective May 7, 1993.

ITEM XX

INFORMATION REGARDING FRANCHISES OF THE COMPANY

For the period:	01-01-90 — 12-31-90	01-01-91 — 12-31-91	01-01-92 — 12-31-92	01-01-93 — 04-30-94
Number of Existing Locations Sold	1	3	2	0
Number of New Franchised Locations Opened	0	3	4	1
Number of Company-owned Locations Opened	0	0	0	0
Number of Franchised Locations Closed	23	20	37	6
Number of Company-owned Locations Closed	4	2	0	0
Total Number of Franchised and Company–owned Locations Open at End of Each Period	250	231	198	193

As of April 30, 1993, there were 189 franchised Wicks 'N' Sticks locations in operation. The name of the franchisee, the business address, and the business telephone number for each franchisee is attached hereto as Exhibit "A".

As of April 30, 1993, there were four (4) Company-owned Wicks 'N' Sticks locations in operation of a type substantially similar to those offered by this offering circular. The business address and telephone number, if applicable, for each location is attached as Exhibit "B".

As of April 30, 1993, the Company executed one (1) franchise agreement for a Wicks 'N' Sticks location which was not then in operation.

Wicks 'N' Sticks Uniform Franchise Offering Circular
Effective May 7, 1993.

During the one (1) year period following the date of this offering circular, the Company estimates that Wicks 'N' Sticks franchises will be sold or granted in the following states:

State	Number of Franchises
California	3
Florida	2
Georgia	1
Illinois	1
Oklahoma	1
Maryland	1
Texas	1
Washington	1
Total	11

This is an estimate only and is subject to, and dependent upon, economic conditions, financing availability, location of sites acceptable to the Company, and other factors.

For the period:	01-01-90 — 12-31-90	01-01-91 — 12-31-91	01-01-92 — 12-31-92	01-01-93 — 04-30-94
1. Franchise Cancellations and Terminations for:				
a. Failure to comply with quality control standards	0	0	0	0
b. Other Reasons				
1. Failure to comply with the terms of the Franchise Agreement	7	13	27	0
2. Leases expired or were terminated by mutual agreement between the Company, the Franchisee, and the Lessor	0	12	9	6
2. Franchise not renewed by the Franchisee	0	1	1	0
3. Reacquisitions:				
a. Through purchase by the Company	0	0	0	0
b. Otherwise	2	4	1	0

The names, last known addresses, and telephone numbers of every Wicks 'N' Sticks franchisee in the United States whose franchise has, within the twelve (12) month period immediately preceding the effective date of this offering circular, been terminated, canceled, not renewed, or who has, during the same time period, otherwise voluntarily or involuntarily ceased to do business pursuant to their Franchise Agreement are listed below. The franchisee may still be doing business pursuant to one (1) or more other Franchise Agreements with the Company.

Name	Last Known Address	Telephone Number

(Omitted, but the Complete List Would Follow Here and on Additional Pages)

EXHIBITS

The following exhibits have been omitted for this printing, but would normally be next in this offering circular.

EXHIBITS:

A-1   FRANCHISED WICKS 'N' STICKS LOCATIONS

B-1   COMPANY-OWNED WICKS 'N' STICKS LOCATIONS

C-1   FINANCIAL STATEMENTS

D-1   FRANCHISE AGREEMENT

ASK YOURSELF

► If the next time you see an offering circular you'll know what you're looking for and why.

► If you know how to compare the disclosure document and the franchise agreement for consistency.

TOTAL PREPARATION WITH WORKSHEETS AND EVALUATIONS: Make Your List and Check It Twice

THE RIGHT STUFF

"No great thing is created suddenly, any more than a bunch of grapes or a fig. If you tell me that you desire a fig, I answer you that there must be time. Let it first blossom, then bear fruit, then ripen."

—Epictetus

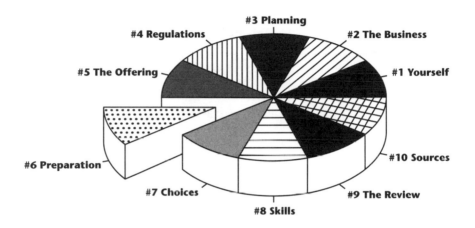

So, you think you're ready to be a franchise owner. Perhaps you are. But first, we'd like you to do another self-evaluation to ensure your readiness.

Be completely honest as you answer the questions on the next few pages. You did a good assessment in Chapter One, but now you have more information to work with and the questionnaire is more intense.

Take your time and note any areas you need time to work on before moving toward a franchise purchase.

ARE YOU READY? — AN ASSESSMENT

Checklist for Financial Suitability

1. Have you and your spouse discussed the pros and cons of going into business for yourselves? *Answer:* _____

2. Are you in complete agreement? *Answer:* _____

3. Will your savings be enough for at least one year after you have paid for the franchise? *Answer:* _____

4. Will the possible loss of company benefits including retirement plans be a problem down the road? *Answer:* _____

5. Are you and your spouse ready to make the necessary sacrifices in the way of money and time in order to operate a franchise? *Answer:* _____

6. Do you have the financial resources required to obtain the franchise you really want? If not, where are you going to get the capital? *Answer:* _____

7. Do you have a written balance sheet of your assets and liabilities? *Answer:* _____

8. Do you realize that most franchises generally do not break even for at least one year after opening or longer? *Answer:* _____

9. Do you have additional sources of financing that you could consider if your first choice doesn't work? *Answer:* _____

10. Will one of you remain employed at your current occupation while the franchise is in its initial, pre-profit stage, and can you manage the business this way? *Answer:* _____

Checklist for Personal Suitability

1. Are you prepared to give up some independence in exchange for the advantages the franchise offers you with hard work and regulations? *Answer:* _____

2. Have you and your spouse had recent physicals and can you handle physical demands? *Answer:* _____

3. Are you and your spouse physically able to handle the strain involved in operating a franchise caused by long hours and possible stress? *Answer:* _____

4. What is the present state of your health? *Answer:* _____

5. Have you examined the franchise you desire and truthfully concluded that you would enjoy running it for years or until retirement? *Answer:* _____

6. Will your family members, particularly small children, suffer from your absence while you build up your business and work long hours? *Answer:* _____

7. Do you have the ability and people skills to work smoothly and profitably with your franchisor, your employees and your customers; are you a people person? *Answer:* _____

8. Do you have a capable person to take over the business if you become ill? *Answer:* _____

9. Have you asked your friends and relatives for their candid opinions as to your emotional, mental, and physical suitability for running a franchise? *Answer:* _____

10. Do you enjoy working with others and getting involved? *Answer:* _____

11. If the franchise is in a new location, do you realize that it would be beneficial to you, in most instances, not to sell your home and buy a new home in a new area until the business is operating at a profit? *Answer:* _____

Checklist for Business Suitability

1. Is it possible for you to become employed in the type of business you seek prior to any purchase, so you can learn the business? *Answer:* _____

2. Have you conducted independent research on the market you are contemplating entering?
    Answer: _____

3. Do you have management experience in business that will help you run the franchise you'll buy?
    Answer: _____

4. Have you determined whether the product or service you propose to sell has a market in your prospective territory or is there more than enough competition?
    Answer: _____

5. If you have made your choice of franchises, have you researched the prospective franchisor?
    Answer: _____

6. What will the market for your product or service be like three years from now? *Answer:* _____

    _____

    What competition exists in your area already?
    Answer: _____

    _____

Checklist for Other Considerations

1. Have you prepared a business plan for the franchise of your choice? *Answer:* _____

2. Do you know an experienced franchise attorney who can evaluate the franchise contract you are looking into? *Answer:* _____

3. Do you know an experienced accountant you'll work with? *Answer:* _____

DON'T BE SHY

If you think you're ready to own your first franchise, you're ready to start the interviewing process. You may have one franchise operation in mind or you may be considering several to talk to. We mentioned earlier in this book the importance of doing your homework and asking questions. We also briefly discussed the importance of talking directly with the current franchisees of the franchisor that you have an interest in.

Use the following forms for each interview you go on. They will help guide you through your evaluation. Be honest and open with the franchisees you interview. It is very important to know how they feel about their business before you sign up.

CONDUCTING THE FRANCHISE INTERVIEWS

What to Ask Existing Franchisees

1. How long did it take you to break even?

_____

2. Was the training you received as useful as the franchisor promised?

_____

3. Are your actual costs the same as or close to that stated in the Offering Circular?

_____

4. Is the product or service you sell in demand and respected?

_____

5. Are goods from the franchisor on time and of good quality?

_____

6. Has the business made the profit you expected it to make and is it enough to continue on?

_____

7. Are you happy with the abilities of the franchisor?

_____

8. In what areas could they improve the training?

_____

9. Does the franchisor listen to your concerns and help when they can?

_____

10. What disputes have you had with your franchisor that have hurt the operations?

_____

11. Have you had disputes that you did not settle with the franchisor?

_____

12. When did they settle and how?

_____

13. Is your franchise profitable and how soon did it become profitable?

_____

14. Is your franchisor friendly and helpful to work with?

_____

15. Do you know of any problems the franchisor has had with other franchisees or anyone in business? If so, what was the problem and how was it handled?

_____

16. Are you satisfied with the advertising assistance the franchisor has provided?

_____

17. Have the operations manuals helped you? What do you think of the material in the manual? Are the manuals changed and kept current?

You Have a Right to Know

We stated earlier that many of your questions will be answered once you receive a copy of the offering circular and the contract. Prior to that you'll want to be prepared for your meetings with the franchisor. You'll want to know what to look for in the documents and to have your questions and considerations outlined. Use the questionnaire on the following pages to help you through that process.

Remember, never let any question you have for the franchisor go unanswered.

Conducting Franchisor Interviews: Information to Obtain from the Franchisor

1. Does the franchisor have information regarding actual, average, or forecasted sales?

Answer: _____

2. Does the franchisor have information regarding actual, average, or forecasted profits?

Answer: _____

3. Does the franchisor have information regarding actual, average, or forecasted earnings?

Answer: _____

4. What information have you received?

Answer: _____

5. What is the total investment of the franchise?

Answer: _____

6. What are the initial franchise fees used for?

Answer: _____

7. Will the franchisor require any other fees? If so, what are they?

Answer: _____

8. Does the franchisor provide financing? If so, what are the terms?

Answer: _____

9. Will the franchisor lease space to you? *Answer:* _____

10. Do they assist you in a location for your franchise operation?

Answer: _____

11. How long has the company been in business?

Answer: _____

12. Is the franchisor a corporation with experienced management?

Answer: _____

13. Is the franchisor a small or large company?

Answer: _____

14. Is the franchisor offering you exclusive territory? If yes, for how long?

Answer: _____

15. What do you know about the franchise area offered you?

Answer: _____

16. Can the franchisor sell additional franchises in your territory?

Answer: _____

17. Who has the right of first refusal?

Answer: _____

18. Will the franchisor provide you with earnings of existing franchisees?

Answer: _____

19. Will the franchisor provide you with their names and locations?

Answer: _____

20. Are there requirements for purchasing or leasing goods or services from the franchisor or other designated sources?

Answer: _____

21. What kind of training does the franchisor provide for you?

Answer: _____

22. Are there any restrictions on what and the way franchises may sell? If so, what are they?

Answer: _____

23. Are there regulations and restrictions for hiring personnel?

Answer: _____

24. What does the contract state regarding termination, modification, and renewal conditions of the franchise agreement?

Answer: _____

25. Under what conditions can you terminate the franchise contract?

Answer: _____

26. Does your prospective franchisor allow variances in the agreement for some of his other franchisees?

Answer: _____

27. What happens if you decide to cancel the contract and what time frames apply?

Answer: _____

28. Are there any federally registered trademarks, service marks, trade names, logotypes and/or symbols associated with the franchise?

Answer: _____

29. Are you, as a franchisee, entitled to use them in all areas including local advertising?

Answer: _____

30. If you sell your franchise back to your franchisor under the right of first refusal, what are the conditions?

Answer: _____

31. Are there existing patents and copyrights on products or services?

Answer: _____

32. What is the background experience and achievement records of key management and owners of the operation?

Answer: _____

33. Are there endorsement agreements for advertising purposes? If so, what are the terms and how will they benefit you?

Answer: _____

34. Has the franchisor investigated you or do they just want the money?

Answer: _____

35. How successful is the franchise operation? (Use Dun & Bradstreet reports, magazine articles, etc., to supplement information the franchisor gives you.)

Answer: _____

36. Has the franchisor complied with FTC and state disclosure laws?

   Answer: _____

37. What is the franchisor's history in relation to past litigation or prior bankruptcies? (Do your own checking.)

   Answer: _____

38. Are the financial statements the franchisor gave you official?

   Answer: _____

39. Does the company have a reputation for honesty and fair dealing among all business associates?

   Answer: _____

40. Exactly what does the franchisor provide for you that you cannot provide for yourself?

   Answer: _____

THE FRANCHISE APPLICATION

Once you've chosen a franchise, done your homework and feel ready to get down to business, it will be time to see if the franchisor really wants you in their operation. As we stated earlier, a reputable franchisor will look as closely at you as you have looked into their history. Most good franchise operations are quite selective, and it takes some work on your part to become a franchisee even if you have the required capital.

Franchise application forms vary but most will require details about you and your family, your experience in business, and your finances. You should take the same approach as you would on a financial application and proposal: that is, give as much valuable information as you can. Take your time with each form they give you and leave nothing blank. Take a look at the following pages of what you may be expected to fill out.

What You Can Expect To See When You Receive a Franchise Business Application

FRANCHISEE BUSINESS APPLICATION

Name of Franchisor and Franchise: _____ Date: _____

Name of Franchisee: _____

Personal Information:

❑ Single   ❑ Separated   ❑ Married   ❑ Divorced

Number of Minor Children: _____ Ages of Children: _____

Other Dependents: _____

❑ Own/Buying Home   ❑ Rent   ❑ Live with Parents

    ❑ Live with Spouse   ❑ Live with Relatives

Mortgage or Rental Payments: $_____ /month

    If buying, monthly payments: $_____ Paid to: _____

Applicant:

Name: _____   Address: _____

                                                      City/St/Zip: _____

Home Phone: _____   Business Phone: _____

Social Security #: _____   Birthdate: _____

Education: _____   Last Grade Completed: _____

College/University: _____   Major/Minor: _____

Degree Received: _____   Year Degree Received: _____

Partners or Applicant's Spouse (if applicable):

Name: _____   Address: _____

City/St/Zip: _____

Home Phone: _____   Business Phone: _____

Social Security #: _____   Birthdate: _____

Past Employment of Applicant:

Current Employer: _____

Address: _____

City/St/Zip: _____

Position: _____   Present Salary: _____

Started (Year) _____ to _____

Description of Work: _____

Prior Employer: _____

Address: _____

City/St/Zip: _____

Position: _____   Present Salary: _____

Started (Year) _____ to _____

Description of Work: _____

Have you ever owned your own franchise or any type of business?

Business Name: _____   How long owned? _____

Address: _____   How many employees: _____

Type of business: _____

Describe how the business changed over the time you owned it. What happened to it? _____

_____

_____

Business Name: _____ How long owned? _____

Address: _____ How many employees? _____

Type of business: _____

Describe how the business changed over the time you owned it. What happened
to it? _____

_____

Contacts: _____

Financial Information (Note: Additional financial information may be required upon request.)

Summary

CURRENT ASSETS		CURRENT LIABILITIES	
Checking Account	$_____	Notes Payable	$_____
Savings Account	_____	Amount owed on Real Estate	_____
Total	_____	Total	_____

FIXED ASSETS (SHOW PRESENT VALUE)		LONGTERM LIABILITIES	
Real estate, home *Describe:* _____	$_____		$_____
Other real estate *Describe* _____	_____		_____
Listed stocks & bonds *Describe* _____	_____		_____
Automobile(s) *Describe* _____	_____		_____
Your own business *Describe* _____	_____		_____
Money due you *Describe* _____	_____		_____
Insurance (cash value) *Describe* _____	_____		_____
Other assets *Describe* _____	_____		_____
Total	_____		_____

Total Assets: $_____   Total Liabilities: $_____

Net Worth (assets minus liabilities): $_____

How much capital can you allocate to buy this franchise? _____

If the required amount is not available, how would the investment be obtained?

_____

Do you plan to have a partner? ❑ Yes ❑ No

    If so, will the partner be active? ❑ Yes ❑ No

Do you plan to have investors? ❑ Yes ❑ No

    If so, to what extent? _____

What strategies do you have for obtaining funds? _____

_____

What is the minimum income you need for living expenses annually? _____

From what sources will it come? _____

_____

References

BUSINESS

Name	Address	Years Known
_____	_____	_____
_____	_____	_____
_____	_____	_____
_____	_____	_____

CHARACTER

Name	Address	Years Known
_____	_____	_____
_____	_____	_____
_____	_____	_____
_____	_____	_____

Objectives:

In order of priority, list which specific types of franchises you prefer to become involved with:

1. _____

2. _____

Why are you interested in this particular franchise?

_____

What is your experience in this area?

_____

What are your realistic personal and professional goals three years from now?

_____

Why do you believe you will be able to successfully operate one of our franchises?

_____

Do there appear to be any concerns you have about owning one of our franchises? If so, please state your concerns.

_____

I certify that the enclosed information as given is complete and correct.

_____   _____

Applicant's Signature   Date

A Good Spot Or Not?

Let's say you've progressed as far as your franchise selection. If there are several choices of areas to begin operations, you'll want to do a complete site and territory assessment. A good business site can certainly help your franchise succeed.

It is important to keep your type of business in mind when looking at areas of interest. One type of business product or service may do great in one spot but not another. The following forms will help you take a great deal into consideration when deciding on your franchise location. Remember that some franchisors will have restrictions or requirements already set in the agreement; others will do the site selection themselves.

Your Turn

Answer the following questions:

- ► What locations have I looked at as potential sites for a franchise?

- ► What factors did I use to pick these locations?

- ► Can I accept the franchisor's decision for another location?

SITE AND TERRITORY ASSESSMENT

Franchise Site Assessment

NAME: _____

ADDRESS: _____

_____

PHONE: _____

Date of Report: _____ Address of Potential Site: _____

1. Information on Location and Customers:

    Type of Facility: _____

    Nearest Intersections: _____

    Distance of Nearest Intersections from Facility: _____

    Nearest Street Light and Name of Street: _____

    Description and Allocation of Parking Spaces (front, side and back, as applicable): _____

    Condition of Adjacent Stores: _____

    Amount of Traffic on Streets at Peak Hours: _____

    Description of nearby business, including type of facilities and products or services offered: _____

    _____

2. Customer traffic count of adjacent business or shopping center, if applicable:

    Morning: _____

    Noon: _____

    Evening: _____

3. Major competition in the area:

    Name   Address   Business Type

    _____   _____   _____

    _____   _____   _____

4. Population in the area:

   Population: _____ Year: _____ Increase last 12 mos.: _____%

   Per-Capita Income: $_____ Median Family Income: $_____

   Type of Housing: _____

   Average home/condo/apartment value: $_____

   General comments: _____

   Does this fit your product or service? _____

5. Visibility of site from intersections:

   North _____ South _____ East _____ West _____

   General access: ❏ Excellent ❏ Good ❏ Poor

6. Observations in general:

   Advantages: Disadvantages:

   _____   _____

   _____   _____

   _____   _____

   _____   _____

7. Cost of Purchase or Lease

   Purchase price: $_____ Lease: $_____ Kind of Lease: _____

   Terms of purchase or lease: _____

8. Utility costs that must be paid and estimated amounts:

   _____

   _____

   Description of other costs: _____

   Renewal terms: _____

9. Sign Restrictions

   Freestanding: _____

Exterior: _____

Interior: _____

Will facility owner provide signs if location is a shopping center? _____

10. Other Possible Restrictions

_____

_____

Fire zone: _____ Nearest fire hydrant: _____

Address and distance of closest fire station: _____ ft./miles

Name and location of closest hospital: _____

11. Utility Information

	Company Name	Phone Number
Electric	_____	_____
Natural gas	_____	_____
Water	_____	_____
Telephone	_____	_____
Health Dept.	_____	_____
Zoning	_____	_____
Other:	_____	_____

Problems discovered when contacting utilities: _____

_____

_____

_____

_____

_____

_____

THE OPERATIONS MANUAL . . . YOUR GUIDE TO SUCCESS

Once you've taken the big step, you'll want to know just what to do to get things started. In addition to the training offered by the franchisor, your most valuable tool will be the franchise operations manual.

We encourage you to read it from beginning to end and to keep it handy. It will serve as a valuable tool in running your franchise. When you first enter into the world of franchising, you may not know what to expect. Make yourself familiar with your manual and make sure it has enough information in it to be helpful in the operations of your franchise.

The next few pages give you a glance at what most manuals should and do contain.

What to Expect from an Operations Manual

All franchisors' operating manuals will be unique but most should contain:

1. Introduction
   - Welcoming Letter
   - Biographical Information on Franchisor's Key Management

2. Grand Opening Advice and Guidelines

3. Opening Regulations
   - Preparation by Franchisee with Franchisor's Assistance
   - Setting Dates and Time Periods for
     — Execution of Lease (if applicable)
     — Approval of Lease by Franchisor
     — Site Selection by Franchisee
     — Site Approval by Franchisor
     — Commencement of Facility within Required Number of Days after Execution of Lease (if applicable)
     — Completion of Facility

- Financial Statements

- Necessary Permits and Registration Forms

- Franchisor's Specifications Regarding the Facility

- Equipment, Inventory and Fixtures Needed

- Procurement of Necessary Documents, Items and Services
  — Suppliers
  — Telephone Systems
  — Appropriate Licenses
  — Sales Tax permit
  — Minimum Wage and Equal Opportunity Information
  — Office Forms, etc.

4. Training Procedures

   - Operational Policies

   - Decor and Dress Code of Personnel

   - Customer Service Procedures

   - Delivery Requirements and Techniques

   - Preparation of Sales and Financial Reports, including
     — Business Forms
     — Inventory
     — Preparation of Daily, Weekly and Monthly Financial Statements

   - Security Measures and Safety Requirements

   - Cash Register Operation and Credit Forms

   - Store Policies

   - In-Store Promotion, Advertising, Amendments to Operation Procedures

5. Bookkeeping and Accounting Methods and Close Out

6. Troubleshooting and Contacts

ASK YOURSELF

► What important items should you look for in an operations manual?

► Why are location and site evaluations important before buying a franchise?

► Why should franchisors interview you just as intensely as you interview them? What will they ask on an application form?

FRANCHISE OPPORTUNITIES:
A Business of Your Choice

SO MANY CHOICES

"No one knows what he can do till he tries."
—Publilius Syrus

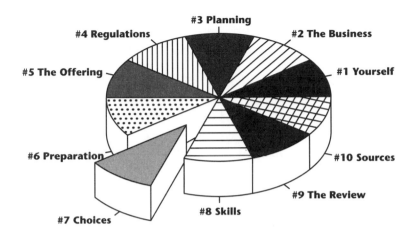

There are many franchise businesses to choose from, but in case you need a sampler and some ideas, we've provided you with a list of some that may catch your interest.

We'll take a look at some franchises that have been established for years and we'll show you some opportunities that may be unknown to you. If you see one that catches your eye, we suggest that you write to the address provided for additional information.

Remember, there are many more franchise opportunities available than the ones you'll see here, so do your research and good luck!

FRANCHISE INFORMATION AND ADDRESSES

Automotive Products/Services

AAMCO TRANSMISSIONS, INC.
One Presidential Boulevard
Bala Cynwgd, Pennsylvania 19004

In Business Since: 1963
Product/Service: Service transmissions for all vehicles.

BRAKE WORLD AUTO CENTERS
2640 Hollywood Boulevard
Hollywood, Florida 33020

In Business Since: 1970
Product/Service: Brakes, alignment, front-end repairs, mufflers
and other repairs.

JIFFY LUBE INTERNATIONAL, INC.
P.O. Box 2967
Houston, Texas 77252-2967

In Business Since: 1979
Product/Service: Offer quick lube for vehicles.

MOBILE TRIM TEAM
1239 Braselton Highway
Lawrenceville, Georgia 30243

In Business Since: 1972
Product/Service: A variety of repair services and complete
upholstery to car dealers, restaurants, motels, hotels, etc.

MUFFLER CRAFTERS, INC.
4911 Birch Street
Newport Beach, California 92660

In Business Since: 1973
Product/Service: A "turnkey" muffler, brakes and front-end
alignment operation.

OIL EXPRESS NATIONAL, INC.
22 Orchard Place
Hinsdale, Illinois 60521

In Business Since: 1979
Product/Service: 10 minute oil, filter and lube service for cars
and trucks.

DOLLAR RENT-A-CAR SYSTEMS, INC.
6141 West Century Boulevard
Los Angeles, California 90045
In Business Since: 1966
Product/Service: Automobile and truck rental.

PAYLESS CAR RENTAL
2350 N. 34th Street
St. Petersburg, Florida 33713
Jay Vahl, President
In Business Since: 1971
Product/Service: Automobile rental.

THRIFTY RENT-A-CAR SYSTEM, INC.
P.O. Box 35250
5330 East 31st Street
Tulsa, Oklahoma 74153-0250
In Business Since: 1950
Product/Service: Automobile renting and leasing.

Beauty Supplies and Salons

CUSTOM CUTS, INC.
13850 Manchester Road
St. Louis, Missouri 53011
In Business Since: 1985
Product/Service: Family hair care.

FAMILY HAIRCUT STORE
398 Hebron Avenue
Glastonburg, Connecticut
In Business Since: 1985
Product/Service: Hair care for families - no appointment needed.

FANTASTIC SAM'S, THE ORIGINAL FAMILY HAIRCUTTERS
3180 Old Getwell Road
P.O. Box 18845
Memphis, Tennessee 38181-0845
In Business Since: 1974
Product/Service: Retail hair care.

HAIR CRAFTERS
125 South Service Road
P.O. Box 265
Jericho, New York 11753

In Business Since: 1955
Product/Service: Full service hair care salons.

LORD & LADY'S HAIR SALONS
450 Belgrade Avenue
Boston, Massachusetts 02132

In Business Since: 1971
Product/Service: Professional hair care; full service salons.

SNIP 'N CLIP
6804 West 75th Street
Overland Park, Kansas 66212

In Business Since: 1982
Product/Service: Family haircuts.

SUPERCUTS
555 Northgate Drive
San Rafael, California 94903

In Business Since: 1975
Product/Service: Custom hair care.

Business Services

AMERICAN ADVERTISING DISTRIBUTORS, INC.
234 South Extension Road
Mesa, Arizona 85202

In Business Since: 1976
Product/Service: Trademarked techniques for direct mail
  business.

AMERICAN POST 'N PARCEL, INC.
315 West Pondera Street, Suite F
Lancaster, California 93534-3681

In Business Since: 1986
Product/Service: Packaging and shipping parcels.

ANSWERING SPECIALISTS
119 West Doty Avenue
Summerville, South Carolina 29483

In Business Since: 1989
Product/Service: Real person telephone answering service.

COMPREHENSIVE ACCOUNTING CORPORATION
2111 Comprehensive Drive
Aurora, Illinois 60505

In Business Since: 1949
Product/Service: Computerized accounting to businesses of
   all types.

FASTSIGNS
4951 Airport Parkway, Suite 530
Dallas, Texas 75248

In Business Since: 1985
Product/Service: High-tech, computerized, retail sign stores.

H & R BLOCK, INC.
4410 Main Street
Kansas City, Missouri 64111

In Business Since: 1955
Product/Service: Income tax preparation and electronic filing.

HOMEWATCH CORPORATION
2865 South Colorado Boulevard
Denver, Colorado 80222

In Business Since: 1973
Product/Service: Homesitting and attentive care service.

THE LETTER WRITER, INC.
9357 Haggerty Road
Plymouth, Michigan 48170

In Business Since: 1981
Product/Service: Trademarks and logos in connection with
   writing service, answering service, etc.

NETWORK BUSINESS SERVICES, INC.
3003 G. Greentree Executive Campus
Marlton, New Jersey 08053

In Business Since: 1988
Product/Service: Retail office and shipping center.

Construction/Remodeling Materials and Services

BATHCREST, INC.
2425 South Progress Drive
Salt Lake City, Utah 84119

In Business Since: 1979
Product/Service: Specializing in porcelain resurfacing of
    bathtubs, sinks, ceramic wall tile, etc.

CALIFORNIA CLOSET CO.
21300 Victory Boulevard, Suite 1150
Woodland Hills, California 91367

In Business Since: 1979
Product/Service: Custom closet installation.

EXOTIC DECKS, INC.
5005 Veterans Memorial Highway
Holbrook, New York 11741

In Business Since: 1989
Product/Service: Exotic decks.

KITCHEN SAVERS, INC.
715 Ross Street
La Cross, Wisconsin 54603

In Business Since: 1982
Product/Service: Remodels kitchen cabinets.

PERMA-GLAZE, INC.
1200 North El Dorado Place, Suite A-110
Tucson, Arizona 85715

In Business Since: 1978
Product/Service: Restoration and refinishing of bathroom and
    kitchen fixtures.

Cosmetics

JUDITH SANS INTERNATIONALE, INC.
3853 Oakcliff Industrial Court
Atlanta, Georgia 30340
In Business Since: 1969
Product/Service: Makeover centers and complete cosmetic line.

SYD SIMONS COSMETICS, INC.
2 East Oak Street
Chicago, Illinois 60611
In Business Since: 1940
Product/Service: Makeup and skin care studio, cosmetic products and accessories.

Donut Shops

THE DONUT HOLE
Rt. 1, Box 704
Dickinson, North Dakota 58601
In Business Since: 1976
Product/Service: Sit-down and take-out donuts and other baked products.

TASTEE DONUTS, INC.
5600 Mounes Street
Harahan, Louisiana 70123
In Business Since: 1965
Product/Service: Donuts and other baked goods.

Grocery and Specialty Stores

BARNIE'S COFFEE & TEA COMPANY, INC.
340 North Primrose Drive
Orlando, Florida 32803
In Business Since: 1980
Product/Service: Gourmet coffee and tea store with other specialty items.

LE CROISSANT SHOP
d/b/a BLUE MILL ENTERPRISES CORP.
227 West 40th Street
New York, New York 10018

In Business Since: 1981
Product/Service: Authentic French baked goods.

CHEESECAKE, ETC.
400 Swallow Drive
Miami Springs, Florida 33166

In Business Since: 1974
Product/Service: Eat in or take home cheesecake and other
    specialty desserts.

THE COFFEE MERCHANT
Box 2159
Sand Point, Idaho 83864

In Business Since: 1979
Product/Service: Fine teas, coffees and related items.

COOKIE FACTORY OF AMERICA
651 East Butterfield Road, Suite 503
Lombard, Illinois 60148

In Business Since: 1974
Product/Service: Quality popular baked goods.

DIAL-A-GIFT, INC.
2265 East 4800 South
Salt Lake City, Utah 84117

In Business Since: 1980
Product/Service: National gift wire service delivering gift baskets
    with fresh fruit, gourmet foods, wines and other special
    items inside.

GLASS OVEN BAKERY
1640 New Highway
Farmingdale, New York 11735

In Business Since: 1977
Product/Service: Bakery/cafe where all baked goods are baked in
    full view of the customers.

GREAT EARTH VITAMIN STORES
175 Lawman Lane
Hicksville, Wyoming 11801

In Business Since: 1971
Product/Service: Extensive line of quality vitamins.

HEAVENLY HAM
8800 Roswell Road, Suite 135
Atlanta, Georgia 30350

In Business Since: 1984
Product/Service: Specializes in spiral sliced, fully baked, honey
    and spiced-glazed hams.

MRS. POWELL'S CINNAMON ROLLS
500 Franklin Village Drive, Suite 106
Franklin, Massachusetts 02038

In Business Since: 1984
Product/Service: Cinnamon rolls, gourmet sandwiches, muffins,
    soups, salads and other homemade products.

MY FAVORITE MUFFIN
15 Engle Street, Suite 302
Englewood, New Jersey 07631

In Business Since: 1987
Product/Service: Specialty baked goods, gourmet muffins and
    over 120 varieties of privately labeled gourmet coffee and
    frozen yogurt.

THE ORIGINAL GREAT AMERICAN CHOCOLATE CHIP
    COOKIE CO., INC.
4685 Frederick Drive
Atlanta, Georgia 30339

In Business Since: 1977
Product/Service: Retail cookie stores.

Restaurants/Drive-ins/Carry-outs

ARTHUR TREACHER'S INC.
5121 Mahoving Avenue
Youngstown, Ohio 44515

In Business Since: 1969
Product/Service: Operation of fish & chips restaurants.

BAGEL NOSH, INC.
247 West 12th Street
New York, New York 10014

In Business Since: 1973
Product/Service: Manufacturing of bagels and the sale of
   delicatessen foods.

BACALLS CAFE FRANCHISES, INC.
6118 Hamilton Avenue, Suite 200
Cincinnati, Ohio 45224

In Business Since: 1982
Product/Service: Full service restaurant and bar.

BOZ HOT DOGS
770 East 142nd Street
Dolton, Illinois 60419

In Business Since: 1969
Product/Service: Fast food carry-out.

CALIFORNIA SMOOTHIE
1700 Route 23
Wayne, Wisconsin 07470

In Business Since: 1973
Product/Service: Healthy foods and frozen yogurts.

CAPTAIN D'S—A GREAT LITTLE SEAFOOD PLACE
1727 Elm Hill Pike
Nashville, Tennessee 37210

In Business Since: 1969
Product/Service: Quick service seafood restaurant.

CHILI GREAT CHILI, INC.
215 West Franklin Street, Suite 307
Monterey, California 93940
In Business Since: 1984
Product/Service: Restaurant, chili served in hundreds of ways.

CORN DOG 7, INC.
P.O. Drawer 907
Hughes Springs, Texas 75656
In Business Since: 1978
Product/Service: Restaurant specializing in corn dogs.

HARTZ KRISPY CHICKEN
d/b/a HARTZOG, INC.
14409 Cornerstone Village Drive
Houston, Texas 77014
In Business Since: 1972
Product/Service: Chicken and side orders in a fast food
   operation.

JERRY'S SUB SHOP
15942 Shady Grove Road
Gaithersburg, Maryland 20877
In Business Since: 1954
Product/Service: Subs and pizza; beer and wine served.

KETTLE RESTAURANTS, INC.
d/b/a KETTLE RESTAURANTS
P.O. Box 2964
Houston, Texas 77252
In Business Since: 1968
Product/Service: Family restaurants operating 24 hours/day.

LITTLE CAESAR ENTERPRISES, INC.
2211 Woodward Avenue
Detroit, Michigan 48201
In Business Since: 1959
Product/Service: Pizza.

LONG JOHN SILVER'S INC.
JERRICO, INC.
P.O. Box 11988
Lexington, Kentucky 40579

In Business Since: 1969 (Long John Silver's founded)
Product/Service: Fast food seafood restaurants.

THE PASTA HOUSE COMPANY FRANCHISES, INC.
1924 Marconi
St. Louis, Missouri 63110

In Business Since: 1967
Product/Service: Italian foods and gourmet pastas in a family
atmosphere.

PEPE'S INCORPORATED
1325 West 15th Street
Chicago, Illinois 60608

In Business Since: 1967
Product/Service: Mexican food restaurants.

Health Services/Products

FORTUNATE LIFE WEIGHT LOSS CENTERS
P.O. Box 5604
Charlottesville, Virginia 22905

In Business Since: 1984
Product/Service: Supervised weight control program.

GENERAL NUTRITION FRANCHISING, INC.
921 Penn Avenue
Pittsburgh, Pennsylvania 15222

In Business Since: 1939
Product/Service: Products, services and information for better
health.

JAZZERCISE, INC.
2808 Roosevelt Street
Carlsbad, California 92008

In Business Since: 1974
Product/Service: Dance fitness programs.

JENNY CRAIG INTERNATIONAL, INC.
445 Marine View Avenue, Suite 300
Del Mar, California 29014

In Business Since: 1983
Product/Service: Weight loss and nutritionally balanced menus.

WOMEN'S WORKOUT WORLD
5811 West Dempster
Morton Grove, Illinois 60053

In Business Since: 1968
Product/Service: Women's health and fitness club.

Home Furnishings

DECO HOME STORES, INC.
P.O. Box 1586
Placerville, California 95667

In Business Since: 1983
Product/Service: Carpets, window coverings, wallpaper, etc.

THE DRAPERY FACTORY FRANCHISING CORP.
80 Tanforan Avenue, Suite 10
South San Francisco, California 94080

In Business Since: 1980
Product/Service: Retailer of custom window coverings.

THE FLOOR TO CEILING STORE
4909 Highway 52 North
Rochester, Minnesota 55901

In Business Since: 1981
Product/Service: Home and office interior products.

JOHN SIMMONS GIFTS
36 West Calhoun
Memphis, Tennessee 38103

In Business Since: 1960
Product/Service: Home furnishings and unique gifts.

STEAMATIC INCORPORATED
1601 109th Street
Grand Prairie, Texas 75050

In Business Since: 1948
Product/Service: Cleaning and restoration services.

WINDOW WORKS, INC.
2101 N.W. 33rd Street, Suite 300A
Pompano Beach, Florida 33069

In Business Since: 1978
Product/Service: Custom interior window treatments.

Home Cleaning Services

HOME CLEANING CENTER OF AMERICA
11111 West 95th Street, Suite 219
Overland Park, Kansas 66214

In Business Since: 1981
Product/Service: Residential home cleaning service.

MERRY MAIDS
1117 Mill Valley Road
Omaha, Nebraska 68154

In Business Since: 1980
Product/Service: Professional home cleaning.

MOLLY MAID, INC.
707 Wolverine Tower Building
3001 South State Street
Ann Arbor, Michigan 48108

In Business Since: 1978
Product/Service: Professional home cleaning.

Optical Services and Products

NUVISION, INC.
2284 South Ballenger Highway
Flint, Michigan 48503

In Business Since: 1956
Product/Service: Optical products and accessories.

PEARLE VISION CENTERS
2534 Royal Lane
Dallas, Texas 75229

In Business Since: 1962
Product/Service: Optical retail outlets.

TEXAS STATE OPTICAL (TSO)
2534 Royal Lane
Dallas, Texas 75229

In Business Since: 1935
Product/Service: High quality retail optical service by qualified optometrists.

Pet Shops

DOCKTOR PET CENTERS, INC.
355 Middlesex Avenue
Wilmington, Massachusetts 01887

In Business Since: 1966
Product/Service: Retail pets and supplies.

LICK YOUR CHOPS, INC.
50 Water Street
South Norwalk, Connecticut 06854

In Business Since: 1979
Product/Service: Pet products, care and service.

PETNANNY OF AMERICA, INC.
1000 Long Boulevard, Suite 9
Lansing, Michigan 48911

In Business Since: 1983
Product/Service: In home pet care service.

PETS ARE INN, LTD.
27 North Fourth Street, Suite 500
Minneapolis, Minnesota 55401

In Business Since: 1982
Product/Service: Pet boarding.

SHAMPOO CHEZ, INC.
1378 Soquel Avenue
Santa Cruz, California 95062

In Business Since: 1983
Product/Service: Self-serve dog wash.

Printing Services

AMERICAN SPEEDY PRINTING CENTERS, INC.
32100 Telegraph Road, Suite 110
Birmingham, Michigan 48010

In Business Since: 1977
Product/Service: Offset printing, photocopying and other
services.

BUSINESS CARD EXPRESS
2555 South Telegraph, Suite 400
Bloomfield Halls, Michigan 48013

In Business Since: 1982
Product/Service: Business cards and stationery.

BUSINESS CARDS OVERNIGHT
19 6th Road
Woburn, Massachusetts 01801

In Business Since: 1980
Product/Service: Business cards within 24 hours.

Real Estate

ART FELLER AUCTION AND REAL ESTATE COMPANY
Garfield Avenue, Box 267
Cissna Park, Illinois 60924

In Business Since: 1938
Product/Service: Real estate.

BETTER HOMES REALTY
1556 Parkside Drive
P.O. Box 8181
Walnut Creek, California 94596

In Business Since: 1974
Product/Service: Independently owned and operated real estate
offices.

BY OWNER, INC.
Lochanen Square, Suite A
North 8884 Government Way
Hayden Lake, Idaho 83835

In Business Since: 1985
Product/Service: Marketing and real estate services.

CENTURY 21 REAL ESTATE CORP.
2601 S.W. Main Street
P.O. Box 19564
Irvine, California 92713-9564

In Business Since: 1972
Product/Service: Real estate brokerage offices.

RE/MAX INTERNATIONAL
P.O. Box 3907
Englewood, Colorado 80155

In Business Since: 1973
Product/Service: Real estate.

RENTAL SOLUTIONS, INC.
273 West 500 South, Suite 21
Bountiful, Utah 84010

In Business Since: 1983
Product/Service: Super services in the development of rental, commercial, investment and property management.

Travel and Entertainment

ASK MR. FOSTER ASSOCIATES, INC.
7833 Haskell Avenue
Van Nuys, California 91406

In Business Since: 1984
Product/Service: Travel agency.

CINEMA 'N' DRAFTHOUSE, INC.
2204 North Druid Hills Road
Atlanta, Georgia 30329

In Business Since: 1975
Product/Service: Motion picture theatre that serves food.

COMPLETE MUSIC
8317 Cass Street
Omaha, Nebraska 68114
In Business Since: 1974
Product/Service: Disc-jockey entertainment.

CRUISE SHOPPES AMERICA, LTD.
115 Metairie Road, Suite E
Metairie, Louisiana 70005
In Business Since: 1985
Product/Service: Cruise-only travel agency.

EMPRESS TRAVEL FRANCHISE CORPORATION
450 Harmon Meadow Boulevard
P.O. Box 1568
Secaucus, New Jersey 07096-1568
In Business Since: 1957
Product/Service: Travel agency.

GOLF PLAYERS, INC.
5954 Brainerd Road
Chattanooga, Tennessee 37421
In Business Since: 1964
Product/Service: Miniature golf course.

HARTLEY VACATION CENTERS, INC.
508 Reservoir Avenue
Cranston, Rhode Island 02910
In Business Since: 1983
Product/Service: Travel and tour operator.

MINI-GOLF, INC.
202 Bridge Street
Jessup, Pennsylvania 18434
In Business Since: 1981
Product/Service: Pre-fab golf courses.

TRAVEL BUDDY, INC.
P.O. Box 31146
Minneapolis, Minnesota 55431

In Business Since: 1984
Product/Service: Travel service offering assistance for seniors, children and handicapped.

TRAVEL PROFESSIONALS INTERNATIONAL, INC.
10172 Linn Station Road, Suite 360
Louisville, Kentucky 40223

In Business Since: 1983
Product/Service: Travel agency.

UNIGLOBE TRAVEL, INC. (INTERNATIONAL)
1199 West Pender Street, Suite 900
Vancouver, British Columbia
Canada V6E 2R1

In Business Since: 1980
Product/Service: Travel agency.

Art Supplies—Retail

CREATIVE WORLD MANAGEMENT SERVICES, INC.
13450 Farmington
Livonia, Michigan 48150

In Business Since: 1946
Product/Service: Retail art/drafting materials and related items.

DECK THE WALLS
12450 Greenpoint Drive
Houston, Texas 77373

In Business Since: 1979
Product/Service: Retail prints, posters, frames and custom framing.

FAST FRAME U.S.A., INC.
30495 Canwood Street
Agoura, California 91301

In Business Since: 1987
Product/Service: Custom framing and the sale of art.

Florists

BUDDING THE FLORIST, INC.
P.O. Box 491950
Fort Lauderdale, Florida 33309

In Business Since: 1925
Product/Service: Florist shops.

CONROY'S FLORISTS
6621 East Pacific Coast Highway, Suite 280
Long Beach, California 90803

In Business Since: 1960
Product/Service: Full service florist.

FLOWERAMA OF AMERICA, INC.
3165 West Airline Highway
Waterloo, Iowa 50703

In Business Since: 1966
Product/Service: High quality, low price florist.

SILK PLANTS, ETC.
1755 Butterfield Road
Libertyville, Illinois 60048

In Business Since: 1985
Product/Service: Artificial and preserved foliage.

Other Retailing

ANNIE'S BOOK STOP, INC.
15 Lackey Street
Westborough, Massachusetts 01581

In Business Since: 1981
Product/Service: Pre-read, paperback books, new books and
  gift items.

BATHTIQUE INTERNATIONAL, LTD.
Carnegie Place—247 North Goodman Street
Rochester, New York 14607

In Business Since: 1969
Product/Service: Bath, bed and gifts.

CREATE-A-BOOK
6380 Euclid Road
Cincinnati, Ohio 45236
In Business Since: 1980
Product/Service: Creates and sells personalized children's books.

CAT-UPS INTERNATIONAL, INC.
12212 Technology Boulevard
Austin, Texas 78727
In Business Since: 1987
Product/Service: Laser photo sculptures.

EXQUISITE CRAFTS
108 Gleneida Avenue
Carmel, New York 10512
In Business Since: 1973
Product/Service: Craft retailer.

INTILE DESIGNS FRANCHISE SYSTEMS, INC.
9716 Old Katy Road, Suite 110
Houston, Texas 77055
In Business Since: 1976
Product/Service: Imported ceramic tiles, marble and other supplies.

JUST CHAIRS, INC.
446 Francisco Boulevard West
San Rafael, California 94901
In Business Since: 1984
Product/Service: Commercial seating.

MISS BOJANGLES, INC.
9711 Costana Place
Baton Rouge, Louisiana 70815
In Business Since: 1974
Product/Service: Retail jewelry.

THE PERFUMERY, INC.
724 West 21st Street
Houston, Texas 77024
In Business Since: 1983
Product/Service: Reproduction and original fragrances.

SPECIAL SELECTIONS
P.O. Box 3243
Boise, Idaho 83703

In Business Since: 1988
Product/Service: Personal shopping service with sources for
    unique gifts.

WICKS 'N' STICKS DIVISION
WNS, INC.
P.O. Box 4586
Houston, Texas 77210-4586

In Business Since: 1968
Product/Service: Specialty retailer of candles, room fragrance
    products and other home decorating items.

That's all for now.

Your Turn

Complete the following activity:

▶ Choose two or three franchises that interest you and
request a more detailed description of services provided
by the franchise, the number of franchisees, investment
amounts and much more information.

On the next few pages we'll take a look at some franchise
opportunities that you can run out of your home. Generally
you'll find the total investment costs are less than those
franchises requiring a facility.

The advantages and disadvantages are very much the same as
operating any home-based business. If you enjoy working out
of your home, this very well could be the direction you'd like
to take. The following home-based opportunities are not listed
in any particular order.

If you're thinking of running a franchise from home, a few of your choices are . . .

STORK NEWS OF AMERICA, INC.
5075 Morganton Road, #12A
Fayetteville, North Carolina 28314

Product/Service: Newborn announcement service/uses outdoor display signs. Also provides other retail prebirth products.

TRIMARK, INC.
184 Quigley Blvd.
P.O. Box 10530
Wilmington, Delaware 19850-0530

Product/Service: Direct mail marketing company.

ADVANTAGE PAYROLL SERVICES
800 Center Street
Auburn, Maine 04210

Product/Service: Small business payroll services.

KINDERDANCE INTERNATIONAL, INC.
P.O. Box 510881
Melbourne Beach, Florida 32951

Product/Service: Preschool dance programs for skill building.

JANI-KING INTERNATIONAL, INC.
4950 Keller Springs, Suite 190
Dallas, Texas 75248

Product/Service: Commercial janitorial services.

AMERICAN LEAK DETECTION
1750 East Arenas, Suite 7
Palm Springs, California 92262

Product/Service: Residential and commercial water and gas leak detection.

BUTLER LEARNING SYSTEMS
1325 West Dorothy Lane
Dayton, Ohio 45409
Product/Service: Producer and publisher of management
   programs.

THE TAYLOR REVIEW
4806 Shelly Drive
Wilmington, North Carolina 28405
Product/Service: Pre-employment screening.

BETTER BIRTH FOUNDATION
733 Main Street
Stone Mountain, Georgia 30083
Product/Service: Educational courses on the process of
   childbirth.

DEKRA-LITE
17945 Sky Park Circle
Irvine, California 92714
Product/Service: Designing and installing exterior lighting.

RUG DOCTOR PRO
2788 North Larkin Avenue
Fresno, California 93727
Product/Service: Carpet cleaning business.

DECORATING DEN
4630 Montgomery Avenue
Bethesda, Maryland 20814
Product/Service: Shop-at-home decorating service.

ASK YOURSELF

► In what categories of business do I have the greatest interest?

► What franchise opportunity fits my profile?

CHAPTER EIGHT

SKILLS OF THE IDEAL FRANCHISEE: Can You Manage?

SKILL AND QUALITY

"There is always a best way of doing everything."
—Ralph Waldo Emerson

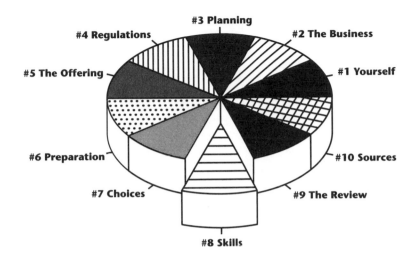

The typical franchise owner will require a multitude of skills. Several years of management experience are quite important. But past "titles" doesn't mean you'll make a good franchisee if your skills haven't been polished enough to be all the things you'll need to be in your new role. The job is vast and you'll need to be all things to many people, such as:

1. A competent learner.

2. A good motivator.

3. A good teacher.

4. Organized.

5. Good at hiring and interviewing.

6. Responsible.

7. Dedicated.

8. Challenged.

9. A good problem-solver.

10. Good at making decisions.

11. An excellent communicator.

12. Good at dealing with conflict and complaints.

13. Capable of following directions.

14. Committed.

15. A great leader.

If you need to brush up on these skills we recommend that you review the following topics in this chapter. If you find that you need to take a refresher course, then you should do so prior to taking on your new venture as franchise owner.

The franchise will be looking for these skills in both your past experience and in your interview with them. The quality franchise organization recruits only the best into their business. You've already devoted some serious thought and time to your self-evaluation. Now it's time to honestly check your skills in order to be a true leader and franchise owner. As you'll see, being your own boss isn't easy but we think that you'll find hard work will bring great satisfaction. So, unless you are just a passive owner, purchasing the franchise as an investor only, you'll be involved in many if not more of the following functions, and we'll offer few tips.

Hiring Employees . . . Go for Quality

Where do you find qualified applicants?

> ► *Advertise in the newspaper:* This is a fast way to receive many résumés but we must tell you that not all those who reply will be qualified. This method is recommended only if you have experience reading between the lines on resumes and you are a skilled interviewer. You'll be busy enough in your business, you won't want to waste time on unqualified applicants. Background checks are time-consuming. Newspaper advertising reaches many but can also be expensive. If you use this

recruiting method be sure you write an excellent ad that explains your needed skills and the applicable requirements.

▶ *Outplacement organizations:* There are many outplacement services today as a result of downsizing. When larger companies reduce their work force, they often provide outplacement services. This can be an excellent source for finding good workers. You'll have access to current employment records and references from recent supervisors. Chances are that you'll find many qualified people.

▶ *Placement/employment agencies:* A large source for qualified employees. You'll find that many employment agencies will do a great deal of the pre-screening for you. We do advise that you check out the agency itself and work only with those of the highest quality and excellent reputations. Don't let their groundwork stop you from doing your own background checks.

▶ *Other employees:* Current employees can be helpful in referring someone for the job. They will know you, your work ethics and the company. This can be helpful because they'll know who will fit the job description over and above others. They will also ask other friends and people they know in business. Word of mouth can generate many responses when you're ready to hire.

▶ *Associations:* Many industry associations have a placement service or a job bank and they can generate applicants well versed in your particular operation. Ask around and you'll be surprised at their willingness to help you out.

▶ *Former employees:* Often employees may leave the work force for one reason or another. They may have been excellent employees but had to leave for a period of time with intent to return to their jobs. These people may need to work part-time because of children at home or other responsibilities. They may be good enough at the job to do it in less time. Don't dismiss giving them the opportunity if it should arise.

▶ *Schools:* High school, colleges, and trade schools can be an excellent source for the hiring of an entry-level position. They may have studied a particular subject that would apply to a position you have.

▶ *State employment agencies:* A free service from the U.S. Employment Service. People who have been retrained and who are eager to work. You can find dedicated people who appreciate the opportunity to work.

ADVICE: Your employees will represent much more than just workers. They are a big part of the image you want your franchise to project. Hire with this in mind. No matter what your business is, you're in business to make money. You're in the business of sales and customer satisfaction. Attracting customers with good advertising is important but will mean nothing if they are not treated with respect, friendliness and given prompt, courteous service. Even the greatest franchise operations with a national reputation cannot hold up or make it today if the employees are rude and thoughtless. Every person in your organization should have sales and service skills. This includes you as manager and owner. Competition is stiff these days and customers return to those places with not only high quality products but also high quality personnel. When you design your job descriptions be sure to include the importance of a great attitude.

Developing a Job Description

Complete this checklist for job description:

- What is the purpose of this job position?
- What is the goal for this position?
- What are the specific job duties?
- Do other duties apply?
- How is the job performed?
- What are the working conditions?
- What procedural standards apply to the job?
- What are the resources?

- What tasks will be performed daily?
- What level of education is required to perform this job?
- What technical skills apply to this position?
- How much past experience is needed to do this job?
- Will additional training be required to perform this job?
- What type of personality will fit best in this position?
- Will this job lead to other opportunities down the road?

Use the following to help you with your job descriptions:

Employment Opportunity:

Job Title: _____

Methods: _____

Knowledge: _____

Duties: _____

Experience: _____

Standards: _____

Personality: _____

Skills: _____

Relations: _____

How Does a Good Manager Create a Positive Company Image?

▶ *Create and Develop Specific Goals*

Written standards establish a target toward which all employees can direct their energy. A clear, concise focus is important. The goals should be reinforced often with each employee.

▶ *Communicate the Desired Image*

Once goals are in place, you must communicate your expectations to all employees. Let everyone know that a standard is set and only this behavior will create a positive image.

▶ *Develop a Means to Measure Results*

Once you've recruited the right people, set standards and trained them, you'll need to know if they're doing their jobs. The best way to find out is through customer feedback. If you have dissatisfied customers, ask why and act on it.*

To ensure that you get the best candidate for the job, you must conduct a thorough interview. To do so . . .

1. Ask many questions. Open-ended questions create detailed answers.

2. Listen for details and for what is not said.

3. Clarify the answers you receive.

4. Ask about beliefs and work values.

5. Question skills.

6. Look for enthusiasm.

7. Look for evidence of being a team player.

8. Look for integrity.

9. Look for ability to communicate.

10. Look for a positive attitude.

11. Look for flexibility and commitment.

12. Look for sincerity and sensitivity.

---

*For an excellent book on this subject, order *Measuring Customer Satisfaction,* by Richard Gerson. Crisp Publications, Inc., Menlo Park, CA 1993.

13. Look for a desire to learn.

14. Look for a good work record.

Your Own Job Description as Owner

Different kinds of businesses require different kinds of skills. At least, they require them in different proportions or mixes. But if we look at the broad range of jobs an owner must perform, we can identify at least the following skills that are common to all:

1. *Professional, functional, or technical skills.*

These can be sales, accounting, clerical, marketing, procurement or any other functions that apply to your business. You may not perform them all but at the least you'll need a working knowledge of all of them to keep the business operating.

2. *Administrative—managerial skills.*

Once again, there are certain elements to all management jobs but the most important are: goal setting, communicating, planning, controlling and implementing. These skills are the backbone of an organization and should not be taken lightly.

3. *Interpersonal skills.*

Your ability to relate to others can make or break a company. Social and behavioral skills that are well-defined can develop and maintain a favorable working atmosphere. It is more than just good human relations.

4. *Business analytical skills.*

In relationship to sales, planning, personal administration, cost control and other functions, the ability to apply basic analytical methods is an absolute necessity.

5. *Problem-solving skills.*

Your ability to think, communicate and take action is extremely important. Every organization experiences problems, whether internal or external, and unless you can use good logic and judgment with these situations, you'll hamper any opportunity for growth. You must be able to look at all aspects of the problem with a clear, objective point of view.

WILL YOU MAKE A GOOD MANAGER?

Your Profile

Answer the following questions:

- Do you know how to set goals and objectives that can be understood?
- Are you the kind of person who will encourage communications and participation?
- Are you a good organizer and planner?
- Are you a good learner, willing to take the time to know all about the company, operations, products and services?
- Are you good at coaching, training, and general support of others?
- Can you give honest and constructive criticism?
- Can you manage a schedule and work with deadlines?
- Can you keep control of many details at one time?
- Do you work well under pressure and complete responsibility?
- Do you know how to delegate?
- Do you know how to foster a team atmosphere?
- Are you a good motivator?
- Can you handle conflict?
- Can you follow procedures and teach others to do the same?
- Do you like working with people?

The above list should help you identify your true abilities to take on the jobs you'll have as manager and owner. If you intend to be an active part of your new franchise business, you'll want to focus on the skills you'll need to keep the business productive and profitable.

Your Turn

Complete the following activity:

▶ If you're currently working, ask others what they think about your ability to manage. If you're not in a management position, ask them if they think you'd qualify and provide them with a checklist so that they can rate you. If you need more feedback, ask friends and family their opinions.

MOTIVATION FOR MANAGEMENT

Some managers and owners may think that employees should be motivated by the simple act of employment and performing their job duties. It would be nice if that's all it took to produce high performance from individuals, but in reality, motivation has to be encouraged, supported and rewarded by management and owners.

In your new role as manager, it is important to not only hire people to do jobs, but to hire those who want to do the job. The owner must understand employees, their jobs, who to reward and how to influence. Creating a motivated team and a positive business culture is certainly easier said than done. Sensitivity to what employees need is paramount to foster a climate that motivates each employee.

Recognizing good work and coaching employees is one of the easiest ways to keep employees excited about their jobs.

The Case of "Not Picture Perfect"

Jack worked for the Photo Flash Company for six months. He was well compensated and was working in a field he loved. Jack slowly started to develop a lack of interest in the store. He developed a negative attitude and would let things slide. The owner finally pointed out to Jack that his performance was not living up to the work he did the first six months on the job, and asked if anything was wrong. Jack politely pointed out that he was glad to know the owner recognized the way he had been performing. Jack's boss set up an employee recognition and reward program shortly after his experience with Jack. Jack went back to excelling in his job.

If you want to kill high performance, simply fail to recognize it and the employee who performed so well.

WHAT'S SO IMPORTANT ABOUT PERSONNEL POLICY?

A few franchisors will provide a personnel policy for your franchise but many do not due to the differences in the law from state to state. But as owner and manager of your franchise, you'll want to have a policy in place and in writing.

Where Do You Begin?

► *The Franchise and the Business*

Introduce your new employees to the franchise, the business, the goals of the company and the history behind the franchise.

► *The Way the Business Operates*

Explain the details of the organization, your working team and the job positions the business requires.

► *Responsibilities*

Describe the responsibilities of each position within the organization and the importance behind them.

► *Compensation and State Laws*

Here you define the compensation for each position. You'll explain the way you pay and not the actual dollars that are given in the employees' agreement. If you offer hourly rate, this is where you'll state that, with the job title. If another position is commission only, you would provide that schedule. Be aware of the Fair Labor Standards Act, the Wage and Hour regulations and State laws. You'll also define overtime and that payment.

► *Business Schedules*
- The business hours your operation will keep, the schedule all employees are to keep and any guidelines that apply are given here.
- Lunch hours plus breaks included.

► *Benefits Offered*
- Medical Insurance
- Vacations
- Leave
- Sick Time
- Holidays Observed

► *Dress Code*
- Uniforms (if applicable)
- Reasonable Standards

► *Personnel Policy*
- Use of Phone
- Visits, etc.

► *Termination*
- Documentation
- Cause
- Behavior
- Discipline

▶ *Performance Reviews*
  - Aspects
  - Time Schedule

▶ *Supplies and Facilities*
  - Availability
  - Use

A Final Word on Managing

Managers should strive to create an organization that keeps morale high and seeks to provide employees with a sense of worth. Actions speak louder than words, so practice the good you preach. Be fair, be sincere, be supportive and above all, be objective in all determinations you make with employees. You'll be rewarded with a dedicated team that will strive to reach organizational objectives.

ASK YOURSELF

► What is "management"? What do managers do?

► Why do so many businesses fail as the result of poor management?

► List the most important skills a manager must have.

► How can "people" make a difference in a business if they foster the right attitude?

CHAPTER NINE

REVIEW AND FINAL COMMENTS: Separating Fact from Fiction

"When you get right down to the root of the meaning of the word 'succeed,' you find that it simply means to follow through."

—F. W. Nichol

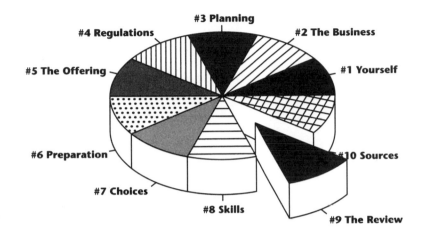

What franchising is . . .

A form of licensing by which the owner (the franchisor) of a product, service or method obtains distribution through affiliated dealers. The service or product that is marketed is identified by name with the franchisor controlling the marketing methods employed. The operation may contain uniform symbols, trademarks, standardized services or products and maintains uniform practices that are outlined in the franchise agreement. A relationship is developed and the franchisor provides the business arrangements with assistance in training, merchandising, procedures, organization, set up and management. The franchisor usually exercises some degree of control. In return, the franchises will share in the reputation developed by the franchisor.

Some of the services franchisees receive for their investment are . . .

1. Initial training.

2. Support with store development.

3. Location analysis.

4. Design and purchases.

5. Continued counseling and training.

6. Advertising support or counsel.

7. Merchandising assistance.

Franchising Works Like This:

Company X develops an idea for a new computerized information system aimed at the legal industry. Company X may or may not expand the business itself, but a good way to expand is for Company X to license the idea together with a defined business package. This package is then offered to entrepreneurs who in turn use their own capital which will expand the business. Company X can charge an initial franchise fee for licensing the brand name and the business package. They will collect a continuing fee based on a percentage of sales called "royalty fees" and may charge additional advertising fees. The Company X business expands with the new businesses, and the entrepreneurs have an opportunity to own their own business with an operations package that will offer a greater probability of success than if the entrepreneur had started the business on one's own.

Remember the Benefits?

1. Buying a franchise gives one the opportunity to own a small business relatively quickly.

2. The identification of an established product with a good name often helps a business reach the break-even point faster than if one started a small business on one's own.

3. A franchisee will also benefit from the franchisor's business experience and expertise.

4. A franchisee buys customer recognition with an established name from the franchisor.

5. Franchisors offer training programs to franchisees which can help the success rate of any business.

6. Quality goods and services are offered at a larger volume-buying power.

7. Many franchisors offer a national advertising program which benefits all the franchisees.

8. Some franchisors will offer limited financial assistance in specific areas, such as purchasing inventory or equipment.

9. Franchisors may offer a franchisee territorial protection within a particular geographic area.

10. Often marketing advice and counseling are offered by the franchisor.

As you've learned, investing in a franchise is not risk-free. The risks of purchasing a franchise are often less than starting a business without all of the help we've listed here. But as you learned earlier, there are some drawbacks and we'll review these now.

Drawbacks:

1. Loss of total freedom due to procedures and control by the franchisor.

2. Turning over a share of the profit to the franchisor and paying other fees.

3. Complying with the written reports a franchisor may demand.

4. Restrictions on the purchase and sale of products.

What Are the Traits and Skills of a Good Franchisee?

The best of the best have . . .

- A certain level of business know-how and savvy with a good understanding of business operations and finance.
- A willingness to work hard and long with a commitment to the business.
- Ability to lead and manage others; train and motivate employees to perform their jobs well.
- A strong desire to succeed.
- Ability to manage money.
- A willingness to please customers.
- Ability to balance many things at one time.

Franchising is not a guarantee of the business making it past the first year of operations. Most businesses fail in their first year because of many poor business and operating decisions. Common sense, hard work, preparation and patience will help the franchisee eliminate some of the risk that could lead to failure.

Potential Franchisees Beware If . . .

- The franchisor tells you not to read the contract and pressures you to sign.
- The franchisor fails to give you a copy of the disclosure document at your first face-to-face meeting.
- There is no operations manual.
- There has been an unusual amount of litigation brought against the franchisor.
- You are discouraged from using an attorney.
- Promises are made but they won't put them in writing.
- Other franchisees have many and the same complaints.

- You are promised high profit with no proof.
- Your questions are not answered to your satisfaction.
- You are not given a complete list of other franchisees to interview.

Remember that you can best evaluate the franchisor by doing your homework. Consult with an attorney and never accept any claims without proof.

What Will You Want to Know? Let's Review . . .

- ► The number of years the franchisor has been in business.
- ► The number of franchise outlets operating.
- ► How many franchise outlets have failed?
- ► What is the total cost of the franchise?
- ► If the franchisor offers a written agreement that covers all details.
- ► What are the conditions and restrictions of the agreement?
- ► If you can ever sell out to a third party.
- ► If advertising and support is offered and for how long.
- ► What happens if you terminate the contract.
- ► If the franchisor offers an earnings claim, with support documents.
- ► If you'll be offered territorial protection.
- ► Your market.

Answer the following questions:

► Are you truly qualified to operate a franchise successfully?

► Do you have the drive, patience, experience, and financial capacity?

► What can the franchisor do for you that you can't do for yourself?

► Are you willing to follow the rules?

► Can you survive the financial risk?

Don't Forget the Disclosure Document

In brief, it covers the following:

1. Identifying information about the franchisor.

2. Business experience of the franchisor's directors and key executives.

3. The franchisor's past business history.

4. Any litigation history of the franchisor and all key people.

5. Bankruptcy history of the franchisor and all key people.

6. Description of the franchise.

7. Money needed for the initial fee and other payments to obtain the business.

8. Any and all continuing expenses that it will take for the franchise to operate.

9. A list of persons with whom the franchisee is required or advised to do business with.

10. Leases, rent or purchases the franchisee will be required to make and all suppliers.

11. Description of compensation or benefits offered by third parties to the franchisor as a result of the required franchisees purchases.

12. Description of any franchisor assistance in financing the purchase of a franchise.

13. The required conduct of business for the franchise.

14. Any required personal participation by the franchisee in the business.

15. Renewal, cancellation and termination of the franchise and all costs for such action.

16. Information about the number of franchises and their rate of termination.

17. Site selection and rights.

18. Training offered.

19. The involvement of celebrity figures.

20. Financial documentation from the franchisor.

The disclosure must include information that is required by the FTC rule. Additional information may be given to the prospective franchisee and should not counter any statements in the disclosure document. Remember, the franchisors must furnish this information but the FTC does not check the document for truth. The FTC's Trade Regulation Rule is designed to help the franchisee evaluate a franchisor and its offerings. The actual contract is the most important consideration for you. It is the agreement between you and the franchisor to enter into business.

Once you receive your list of current franchisees, you'll want to talk with several of them. Interview those who have been in business for several years and in locations that have similar markets to the one you'll be targeting. Ask for their feedback about the franchisor and the business. Remember that there are many questions, but don't forget these few important ones:

1. Are you happy with your investment?

2. Have you had any disagreements with the franchisor? If so, how many were settled to your satisfaction?

3. How long does it take the business to reach a break-even point? How long before you saw a profit?

4. Are you happy with the support you've received from the franchisor?

5. Did the franchisor live up to all his or her promises?

6. Did you receive assistance in opening the business?

7. Has the franchisor done the advertising promised? Has it been effective?

8. Did you receive adequate training? Do your employees receive training?

9. Were the financial projections given by the franchisor accurate?

10. Do you believe this franchise was worth the investment?

Think You'll Need A Loan?

A Review of Some of the Sources . . .

▶ *Small Business Administration*

Makes direct loans only under certain circumstances. SBA does guarantee loans that are made by lenders and banks to qualified applicants.

▶ *Venture Capitalist Groups*

These groups usually demand an equity for their investment and generally have an interest in the large opportunities.

- *Banks*

  Lending policies are restricted. They'll want the loan secured by personal assets or real property in the business.

- *The Franchisor*

  Some offer loan guarantees, few offer direct financing. Most assistance will be secured by your personal assets. Some franchisors have good relationships with banks and can offer assistance.

- *Small Business Lending Companies (SBLC)*

  Companies that are licensed by the Small Business Administration to grant loans for the small business owner.

- *Small Business Investment Companies (SBIC)*

  They focus on equity capital and long-term financing. They are licensed by the SBA. Often require an active role in the management of the business and usually require an equity position.

- *Business and Industrial Development Corporations (BIOC)*

  Underwritten by federal guarantees and often operated by the states. Interest in long-term financing.

- *The Individual Investor*

  Terms will vary but they often want an equity position.

If you'll recall, in order to attract startup money, you'll need a good business and financial proposal. Include the franchisor's offering circular, your résumé, your personal financial statement, and a complete forecast.

To Conclude!

In buying your first franchise, you'll need help from others. A good accountant and a franchise lawyer will save you a great deal of trouble. It is equally as important that you understand the legal language, and decipher the documents along with financial statements for yourself. We hope this book has given you a head start on your quest to be a franchise owner. Our intent is not to encourage or discourage your buying decision but to help you make the right decision. If you should move to buy your first franchise we do hope that you prosper in your franchise venture.

You're probably thinking seriously about your future right now. I'd like to leave you with this one last thought:

"Dreams do come true, but only you can make them happen. First, you must believe in yourself and second, you must believe in the dream."
—Rebecca R. Luhn

GOOD LUCK!

CHAPTER TEN

SOURCES OF
INFORMATION
AND ASSOCIATIONS

SOURCES OF INFOR- MATION

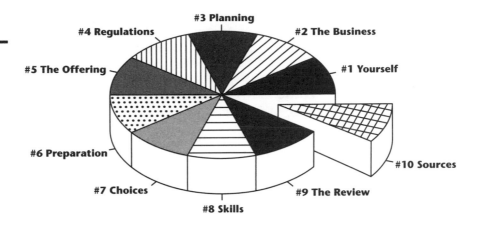

#3 Planning
#2 The Business
#4 Regulations
#1 Yourself
#5 The Offering
#6 Preparation
#10 Sources
#7 Choices
#9 The Review
#8 Skills

Books, Pamphlets, Periodicals, etc.

Checklist for Going into Business. Small Business Administration, Washington, D.C. 20416.

Continental Franchise Review. 5000 S. Quebec, Suite 450, Denver, Colorado 80237.

Directory of Franchise Business Opportunities. Franchise Business Opportunities Publishing Co., Suite 205, 1725 Washington Rd., Pittsburgh, Pennsylvania 15241.

Directory of Franchising Organizations. Pilot Industries, Inc., 103 Cooper St., Babylon, New York 11702.

Financial Security and Independence through a Small Business Franchise. Donald J. Scherer, Pilot Industries, Inc., 103 Cooper St., Babylon, New York 11702.

The Franchise Annual. Info Press, 736 Center Street, Lewiston, New York 14092.

Franchise Encyclopedia. Dr. Alfred J. Modica. Published by ADA Publishing, 28 Sandrock Avenue, Dobbs Ferry, New York 10522.

Franchise Investigation—A Contract Negotiation. Harry Gross and Robert S. Levy. Pilot Industries, Inc., 103 Cooper Street, Babylon, New York 11702.

Franchise World. Franchise Publications, James House, 37 Nottingham Road, London SW 17 7EA, England.

FTC Franchising Rule: The IFA Compliance Kit. International Franchise Association, 1350 New York Avenue N.W., Suite 900, Washington, D.C. 20005.

How to Select a Franchise. Robert McIntosh, International Franchise Association, 1350 New York Avenue N.W., Washington, D.C. 20005.

Investigate Before Investing: Guidance for Prospective Franchisees. Jerome L. Fels and Lewis G. Rudnick. International Franchise Association, 1350 New York Avenue N.W., Suite 900, Washington, D.C. 20005.

Twenty-one Questions. International Franchise Association, 1350 New York Avenue N.W., Suite 900, Washington, D.C. 20005.

Understanding Franchise Contracts. David C. Hjalmselt. Pilot Books, Inc., 103 Cooper Street, Babylon, New York 11702.

The Franchise Advantage. Donald A. Borian and Patrick J. Borian. National Best Seller Corporation, 955 American Lane, Schaumburg, Illinois 60173.

PROFESSIONAL ASSOCIATIONS

You'll find the SBA office nearest to you listed in the white pages of your phone book under U.S. Government. They are an excellent source of small business help. For more information, write:

Small Business Administration
1441 L Street N.W.
Washington, D.C. 20416

They have many regional and district offices.

You'll also find help through some *Trade and Professional Associations:*

American Entrepreneurs' Association
2311 Pontius Avenue
Los Angeles, California 90064

American Federation of Small Business
407 South Dearborn Street
Chicago, Illinois 60605

Small Business Foundation of America
20 Park Plaza
Boston, Massachusetts 02116

ABOUT THE AUTHOR

Rebecca R. Luhn is president of Innovative Consulting Services, a Houston-based training firm. She has been involved in corporate business education for several years, including positions held as director of training for a large health care management firm and for a major airline. Dr. Luhn's interest in business and professional development has resulted in the publication of three books and academic works on file in many universities. Dr. Luhn earned a Ph.D. in Business Communications and also holds the Distinguished Americans award for her contributions to education. She often lectures at Rice University and the University of Houston. In addition to writing, her focus is providing consulting services with a range of expertise in business for both small and large organizations.

NOTES

NOTES

ABOUT CRISP PUBLICATIONS

We hope that you enjoyed this book. If so, we have good news for you. This title is only one in the library of Crisp's best-selling books. Each of our books is easy to use and is obtainable at a very reasonable price.

Books are available from your distributor. A free catalog is available upon request from Crisp Publications, Inc., 1200 Hamilton Court, Menlo Park, California 94025. Phone: (415) 323-6100; Fax: (415) 323-5800.

Books are organized by general subject area.

Computer Series

Beginning DOS for Nontechnical Business Users	212-7
Beginning Lotus 1-2-3 for Nontechnical Business Users	213-5
Beginning Excel for Nontechnical Business Users	215-1
DOS for WordPerfect Users	216-X
WordPerfect Styles Made Easy	217-8
WordPerfect Sorting Made Easy	218-6
Getting Creative with Newsletters in WordPerfect	219-4
Beginning WordPerfect 5.1 for Nontechnical Business Users	214-3

Management Training

Building a Total Quality Culture	176-7
Desktop Design	001-9
Ethics in Business	69-6
Formatting Letters and Memos	130-9
From Technician to Supervisor	194-5
Goals and Goal Setting	183-X
Increasing Employee Productivity	010-8
Introduction to Microcomputers	087-6
Leadership Skills for Women	62-9
Managing for Commitment	099-X
Managing Organizational Change	80-7
Motivating at Work	201-1
Quality at Work	72-6
Systematic Problem Solving and Decision Making	63-2
21st Century Leader	191-0

Personal Improvement

Communications

Small Business and Financial Planning